ARCHITECTURAL DESIGN

EDITORIAL OFFICES:
42 LEINSTER GARDENS, LONDON W2 3AN
TEL: 071-402 2141 FAX: 071-723 9540

EDITOR
Dr Andreas C Papadakis

EDITORIAL TEAM: Maggie Toy (House Editor), Nicola Hodges, Iona Spens
DESIGN TEAM: Andrea Bettella (Senior Designer), Mario Bettella, Jason Rigby
SUBSCRIPTIONS MANAGER: Mira Joka, BUSINESS MANAGER: Sheila de Vallée

CONSULTANTS: Catherine Cooke, Terry Farrell, Kenneth Frampton, Charles Jencks, Heinrich Klotz, Leon Krier, Robert Maxwell, Demetri Porphyrios, Kenneth Powell, Colin Rowe, Derek Walker

SUBSCRIPTION OFFICES:
UK: VCH PUBLISHERS (UK) LTD
8 WELLINGTON COURT, WELLINGTON STREET
CAMBRIDGE CB1 1HZ UK

USA: VCH PUBLISHERS INC
SUITE 909, 220 EAST 23RD STREET
NEW YORK, NY 10010 USA

ALL OTHER COUNTRIES:
VCH VERLAGSGESELLSCHAFT MBH
BOSCHSTRASSE 12, POSTFACH 101161
D-6940 WEINHEIM GERMANY

CONTENTS

Imre Makovecz, Nature Education Centre, Hungary

Zitouna Mosque, Rehabilitation Programme, Kairouan, Tunisia

Mies van der Rohe, Farnsworth House, Illinois

THE LUCINDA LAMBTON DIARY

Ten years ago, even five, if I had dreamt of attending a glitz banquet in honour of car park design, I would have mournfully mocked at the unlikeliness of such an event. Not only have I now seen it, shimmering away under chandeliered glamour, but have also witnessed the astonishing sight of silver 'P's on plinths being presented to the creators of the Country's most elegant car parks. Guzzling smoked salmon, roast beef, Yorkshire pudding and apple tart, we cheered away, raising our glasses to this testament of our ever improving architectural times. With photographs of streamlining at Stansted, the clever pretence of 'grouped buildings' enclosing a multi-storey in Colchester and the amalgamation of countryside and car park at Kynance Cove in Cornwall, we feasted too with delight at the demise of the last bastion of brutalist architecture. The awards, in two categories – urban and rural – are the brainchild of William Davis of The English Tourist Board who has produced lists of Do's and Don'ts for the 'Caring Car Park'. They offer sensible advice; 'Aim to design a car park which is a pleasurable experience for those using it . . . Do not think of the car park as only for cars, rather than for cars and people'. The rural category was won by Downham Village car park in Lancashire, where the glaring metal enemy-the-car has been enclosed in an efficiently serviced area, behind a stone built village. All visual calmness has been restored. Although such perfection often displeases, with feelings that real life has been tidied away. Even Beatrix Potter, the creator of Peter Rabbit and archetypal idealiser of the countryside 'longed to let loose a parcel of sighs' in the model village at Ford in Northumberland, that was built by the Lady Waterford in the 1860s.

Back to the banquet bonanza . . . In the urban category the wrong man, in my view, walked away with the prize; although no stronger criticism than that of being blandly inoffensive could be levelled at the brick towered, dripping with greenery, Bridgefoot multi-storey car park at Stratford Upon Avon. I have already written on these pages of the uncrowned King of the car parks: the avenue de Chartres multi-storey in Chichester and will bore you no further but neither will I offer a hint of apology in writing again and so soon, of such sizzlingly important stop-press architectural news.

For years, ever since my first glimpse of his extraordinary buildings in Hungary, Imre Makovecz has been my golden guru – a distant idol in the architectural field. It was most unlikely that we should ever meet and even if we did, it was sure to be a jabbering Tower of Babel group. The fates, however, were to be fantastically fanciful . . . leading me to prance the night away with my hero in the 30's Beach Ballroom at Aberdeen in Scotland, teaching him the 'Gay Gordons', 'Strip the Willow' and 'The Dashing White Sergeant' as we kneed up. We were at the RIAS (Royal Incorporation of Architects in Scotland) Convention organised to celebrate Scotland's architectural links with Europe

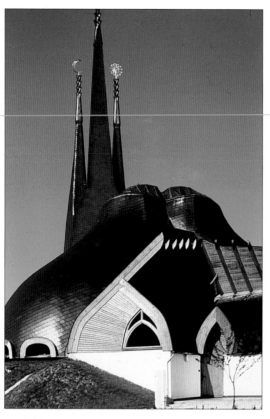

IV

and to forge them further into the future – 'Europe an Architectural Continuum Awakened' was the theme – and all Europe whirled into a merry dance on that circular floor. Vladimir Slapeta, the Dean of the leading school of architecture in Prague was there, so too was Günter Behnisch from Germany and Karl-Dieter Bodack, who has designed Germany's latest train, which boasts a gleaming 30's cocktail lounge. All of them spiritedly a-stepping away with their Scottish hosts.

The convention had begun at Banff, as charming a classical town as could be found anywhere in Scotland or America, the only two countries in my view where Classicism springs straight from the heart, rather than from the head of scholarship. With the grandeur of St Mary's Church of the 1770s and The Court House and County Hall of the 1880s, we were surrounded by the success of Scottish Classicism. The Ionic and Corinthian pilasters of Wilson's Academy (for the advancement of science, literature and the arts) lorded over the town, and there were private houses, big and small (one, described by our doctor guide as 'Quite a nice wee housie') all parading the pride of the place with their crisp and grey stoned classical forms. Duff House, an Adam pile on the outskirts of the town, was quite a different matter and a fancy fairy palace of Baroque Classicism, enriched with domed and cupola'd towers and a wealth of carving, that was built hard by Banff between 1735-49 by William Adam for the Earl of Fife. Rows raged at the time, with Adam never being paid, and the house was never finished. Plans were scrapped for two great wings and Duff House, looking all the taller for being without them, stands with strangely foreign-looking splendour, some hundreds of yards from Banff. So close indeed, that its massively porticoed Doric Temple lodge is now the town's Information Centre and its vinery now stands in a car park that was once obviously the kitchen garden. One of the finest of the town houses in Banff was built, if you please, to take overflow guests from the palatial Duff House.

We were lavishly entertained amid the Baroque splendours which are being painstakingly restored with plans afoot to turn it into a branch of The National Gallery of Scotland. The next morning began with a bang – with the sight of the great mustachioed Makovecz sitting gloomily in the foyer of the shocking 60's Banff Springs Hotel. Notwithstanding the horror of the language barrier, I plunged into praise and we were off, rollicking along on a roller-coaster of talk. With his roars of laughter and rage, there was no hint of a let down in meeting the man behind those passionately Hungarian buildings. The convention progressed apace with eloquent photographs and pleas from Fay Godwin to preserve the countryside for the people. As President of the Ramblers Association, she fights fiercely against government and private policies to fence off walks, as well as against all garbage and signs that ruin the countryside. Günter Behnisch showed us slides of his buildings spanning the years 1952-92, all of them frantic feelers for something new but in my view none of them succeeding in finding it. His latest, a kindergarten, has been given a much needed fillip of humour, which quite saves the day. It was Günter Behnisch though, above all others who spoke like a sage. Vladimir Slapeta was charmingly cheerful, showing us the astonishingly progressive architecture that was being designed in the 20s and 30s in Czechoslovakia.

By this time we were in Aberdeen and surrounded by beauty: the sheer and silvery grey of the granite city encasing every 18th and 19th-century architectural form, gives the sense of such solid satisfaction. Would that today's Scottish architects could live up to this noble tradition. The one cloud – in fact there were several and they were all as black as pitch – was the talks given by the host architectural profession. Their dreariness was a dire disappointment, more especially so as the convention – with such excellent driving forces as Charles McKean, Robin Webster and Joyce Deans – provided them with such a brilliant stage on which to shine. After an afternoon of throwing imaginary rotten eggs at the speakers, the evening began dazzlingly at The City Art Gallery, in its bright, white, classical and granite 'Centre Court'. Although we were not allowed to go into the galleries I felt a knowing cosiness at the knowledge that Lavery's great painting *The Tennis Party* was but a wall away. Upstairs there was another old friend: an immense book-like contraption of gilded 'pages', displaying ovals of the 90 greatest artists of the day, all hauntingly staring at you straight in the face.

With a roar and hug my friend Makovecz was renewed and we thundered on with it to the Beach Ballroom. How did he manage, I asked, to flourish so brilliantly under Communism. Off went my question through the interpreter and back came the answer through the same route – 'Find out for yourself, that was a very stupid and ignorant question!' 'Oh woe' I wailed 'I do feel like a cheap powder puff.' This too went off through the interpreter, this time to set off an arms akimbo explosion . . . WHAT IS A POWDER PUFF!!! Showing him one (a modern nylon version) did little good and with a roar of laughter we danced the night away. At one point we were the only figures on the dance floor, jitterbugging to what he called 'The Chicago Style'. The pictures of his buildings that he showed us the next day held us all spellbound, One after another, Makovecz's churches, houses and halls, magnificently proclaimed the spirit of Hungary, as indeed does their creator. Like great plants rooted in the country, his buildings, with their unimaginably curious forms, are thrusting themselves into the future. It is as if Gaudí, Frank Lloyd-Wright, Charles and Henry Greene, Bruce Goff and Charles Rennie Mackintosh have all been magically merged into one form and sent off soaring to new heights of originality and architectural power. Like plants that writhe and creatures that crawl, with splaying wood and with scale-like tiles, with sharpest spikes and with bulging bodies – their rib cages and vertebrae intact – Makovecz's buildings are as exciting as any that have ever been built, at any time.

Most of them have not been seen in Britain, I was within a hair's breath of a scoop! I asked him if I could have his pictures copied and lo and behold the friendship had been forged enough for him to entrust me with the whole bang lot. Feeling as if I was carrying gold bars I bore the precious burden away to my excellent friend Dave Taylor who frantically copied them throughout the afternoon. An exciting end to an exciting convention in which Scotland triumphed in gathering Europe all around her.

PETER PALUMBO

Interviewed By

MAXWELL HUTCHINSON

The weary postman delivered his back-breaking package to a smart office in the city late in 1964. So started one of the most heroic stories in post-war British architectural history. The massively heavy parcel launched a multi-million pound architectural soap opera which still runs and runs. And, as yet, not a single building in sight. The very special delivery was addressed to Peter Palumbo, a 29-year-old who had recently joined his father's property company on returning from a brief sojourn in New York. To anyone other than Palumbo the contents of the parcel would have been strangely mysterious. Post-marked Chicago, the packaging, packing and labelling was immaculate in every detail. Fit for purpose with nothing left to chance. Off came the hand-made wrapping paper and coarse string, then the closely fitting lid. Out came an ashtray, a complete set of cast bronze door furniture and a simple note in shaky architectural script: 'Is this the sort of thing you have in mind?'

The package, which would have taxed even the logical and inventive genius of Inspector Morse, came from the studio of Mies van der Rohe then bound to a wheelchair, and at 78 within five years of his death. He was completing the National Gallery in Berlin at the end of the Tiergarten, within a stone's throw of the Berlin Wall and the apotheosis of his then world famous International Style and the package containing ashtray and door furniture was his idiosyncratic way of accepting the commission for Mansion House Square.

Palumbo first met Mies in the master's home town of Chicago in July 1962. The ageing genius clearly took a liking to the elegant, cultured, 27-year-old Englishman, whisking him round Chicago in his Lincoln continental convertible and entertaining him after dinner with expansive stories of the heroic period of the Modern Movement and the projects in his office. Mies was to become the godfather of one of Palumbo's daughters by his first wife Denia, who was to die tragically in 1986.

So what was it about the mysterious package addressed to 37a Walbrook? How did an English public schoolboy with an Oxford law degree develop such an intimate relationship with an ex-patriot German architect three times his age? What was this 'thing' Palumbo 'had in mind'? Gentle reader, read on.

Peter Garth Palumbo, who was born on 20 July 1935, is arguably Britain's most important individual post-war architectural patron. Although he describes himself as a property developer there seems little or no 'development' to show for it and certainly not a stick or stone of the development which has won him an Honorary Fellowship of the Royal Institute of British Architects, Chairmanship of the Arts Council of Great Britain, Chancellorship of the new University of Portsmouth and a Life Peerage. The Lord Palumbo of Walbrook who has spent the last 30 years of his life, many millions of pounds and endless dedication on a scheme for the redevelopment of six acres in the City of London, hard up against the Midland Bank by Edwin Lutyens, The Bank of England by John Soane, The Royal Exchange by William Kite, The Mansion House by George Dance the elder and the Church of St Mary Woolnoth by Nicholas Hawksmoor. The Mansion House Square (or Number One Poultry as it is now known) saga, continues to dominate British architectural debate, and all Palumbo has to show for it are two unrealised designs both rendered posthumous by Sir James Stirling's death on 25 June 1992.

To some, the source of the family wealth accumulated by Palumbo's father has seemed obscure, but this is to confuse the character of the man with the nature of his achievement. Peter explains:

My father was an intensely shy person who left school at the age of 14 and was entirely self-educated. He had no social pretensions preferring instead to lead the simple life of a simple man, and he positively loathed publicity. The fact is that my father had a towering genius for property finance which transcended any lack of background or education; and it was that genius that founded the property fortune. In terms of education, he wanted for me everything that life had denied him – a not unknown reaction – which is why I found myself at Eton in 1948, and why we spent regular holidays in Europe where my architectural experience was formed.

Although back home at Eton he was studying modern languages, his Housemaster Oliver van Oss, who was Head of the Modern Language School and deeply steeped in the Arts, seemed to make the biggest impression on the adolescent Palumbo. After the compulsory stint in Chapel on Sunday, Van Oss would gather around him half a dozen carefully chosen boys, including Palumbo, for an impromptu seminar on one of Oss' artistic preoccupations. One such was a pre-prandial chat about Mies van der Rohe.

But neither skill at modern languages, nor an embryonic interest in architecture were to win him a University place. It was games that did it. The distinguished, tall stooping figure of JC Masterman, the Vice-Chancellor of Oxford University, watched Palumbo running for his school and asked him if he would, 'do him the honour of going to his college'. He went up to Worcester College where despite his language background his father insisted that he read law. This joyless subject led him straight back to sport, representing the University at football, rackets and polo and graduating in 1959 with a BA – and needless to say (and probably of more use) a double blue. With the influence of Van Oss lingering on, he took himself off to Greenwich Village, New York and to a job in the department of Master Drawings at the Metropolitan Museum where he had a particular responsibility for 17th-century Italian drawings. Thus the cloisters of Eton and Oxford made way for Greenwich Village in the Swinging 60s.

The taxi driver who collected Palumbo from the airport was instructed to drive straight to 375 Park Avenue. Characteristically, the slobby New York cabby didn't know his street numbers. But he did know the Seagram building. All New Yorkers knew Mies' masterpiece completed in 1958. Palumbo joined the New York Rackets Club immediately opposite the Seagram and watched the latter in the light and shadow of all the New York seasons. But why did this highly-privileged sporting lawyer find the stark simplicity of bronze and tinted glass so clearly beautiful? 'It is so wonderfully understated; an essay in less is more; beautifully proportioned; beautifully detailed; fine materials; well crafted; timeless and serene.' The words of a mature architectural critic, Chairman of the Arts Council

L to R: Mies van der Rohe, The Farnsworth House, Illinois; Le Corbusier, Maisons Jaoul, Neuilly-sur-Seine, Paris; Frank Lloyd Wright, Kentuck Knob, Pennsylvania

of Great Britain no less, but insufficient to explain this particular 24-year-old's unbridled enthusiasm for such an uncompromising example of international modernism. Or for that matter, the embryonic phase of one man's architectural obsession.

The Palumbo family money, which the *Sunday Times* 'Book of the Rich' estimated at around £65 million rendered day-to-day work, in a sense in which most of us understand it , unnecessary. Clearly, the property company had to be run and Peter would eventually take over from his father. But wealth, and an inheritance of that magnitude, must have posed many perplexing problems and posed a myriad of options. Somewhere there had to be a hat peg on which to hang life's ambitions. Cricket, rackets and polo would be all very well for an air-headed dilettante, but Palumbo was, and remains, a great deal more than that. Art, fine 17th-century drawings in the Metropolitan Museum, a great private collection could end up ranking alongside that of the Baron von Thyssen, or, more recently, Charles Saatchi. But there were plenty of great and vastly wealthy men with great and vastly worthy collections of art, most of which would end up as yet another National collection with a personal name tag. Who really wants to join Tate, Clore, or Sainsbury? I should be so lucky.

The graceful, challenging novelty of the Seagram building provided Palumbo with the answer he needed. Why buy half a dozen roomfulls of esoteric canvasses when one class building in the centre of a metropolitan city could bring more personal satisfaction, more public attention and provide by far a greater legacy. After all, his father was already assembling one of the most significant chunks of real estate at the very heart of the City of London at Mansion House Square. Although the buildings were being acquired for their investment value, redevelopment was clearly an option. And then there was just a chance of catching Mies at his drawing board before he died, with the temptation of designing his only building in Great Britain, albeit that it would be a posthumous commission.

Palumbo's father had little time for architects and architecture. He was, however, quickly persuaded by his son's frighteningly simple aphorism, the three M's: Mies Means Money. As Palumbo puts it, 'The Seagram building was then, and has remained ever since, by far the most expensive office building in Manhattan. Usually twice as expensive as any other building in Manhattan . . . because of its reputation and celebrated status'. So much for Architecture? Mies was to be just another real estate pawn on the city chess board. Palumbo journeyed again to Chicago and popped the question. Mies van der Rohe pondered the spiritual subversity of posthumousy. Who would finish the work? Hone the details? Inspect and insist on quality? Just as Mozart had agonised over the final orchestration of a certain Requiem Mass.

Palumbo was very persuasive. He asked the Master if he would design everything; the letter shutes, the ash trays, the door furniture, the internal layouts – everything. It was all to be exactly as Mies would have it. Unlike the Seagram building, the interior of which was separately designed. After a brief site visit in 1964 on the way back from Berlin, Mies despatched the now famous heavy parcel to Walbrook. The message was clear – if you are prepared to spend this much dosh on the hinges and ashtrays then you've got yourself an architect. Palumbo had got his man and made it clear that: 'Commercial considerations were never paramount. We were certainly not going to make a loss on it, but the bottom line in terms of commercial viability was never the deciding factor. It was to build something very good for a very good site.'

Because of complications under the site and the clients' and architect's clear desire, Mies came up with a design for 290 feet of 'Seagram' glass, not far from the City church of Bow Bells. The vast new Mansion House Square was separately designed by Lord Holford who had recently completed a controversial Paternoster Square redevelopment cheek by jowl with St Paul's Cathedral. The rest is now ancient history. There was a public exhibition at the Royal Exchange, which faced the site across Mansion House Square in October 1967. In 12 days, 33,000 visitors voted 73 per cent in favour of Palumbo's proposals. He received support from the London County Council and the City Corporation who resolved that they would grant full Town Planning Consent when: 'The developer had demonstrated that he owned and controlled the site and could enable all the development to continue'. At the time only 60 per cent of the site was in ownership; it took 13 hard and expensive years to collect the rest. Then in 1984, when the architect had been dead for 15 years, after a long and costly Public Inquiry – enter the Prince of Wales.

In the infamous carbuncle speech at the 150th birthday celebrations of the Royal Institute of British Architects, His Royal Highness was not satisfied with the damning reference to the Ahrends Burton and Koralek scheme for the extension to the National Gallery, he fuelled his prejudice with a snipe at Palumbo's precious and personal proposals, '. . . I cannot help thinking how much more worthwhile it would be if a community approach could have been used in the Mansion House Square project. It would be a tragedy if the character and skyline of our capital city were to be further ruined, and St Paul's dwarfed by yet another giant glass stump, better suited to downtown

The World and his aunt had had a go at the site so why not a Royal brick or two!

Chicago than the City of London.' And that from a man who played polo with Palumbo. With friends like that who needs objectors after a closed Public Inquiry?

The world and his aunt had had a go at the site so why not a Royal brick or two. The conservation pressure group, SAVE Britain's Heritage, argued for the retention of the existing Victorian buildings on the site with a scheme commissioned from Terry Farrell. The *Architects Journal* put up a scheme from Campbell Zogolovitch Wilkinson and Gough, designed to stir things up further. 'Their scheme is a characteristically droll offer' said the journal. 'It splits the Mies block down the middle, omits the Square and re-designs the Bucklersbury triangle as a Galleria (in this respect it is not unlike the Farrell scheme)' as Gillian Darley put it in the *Financial Guardian* of May 1984.

By 1985 Palumbo's passionate menage with Mies' last design was over when Secretary of State, Patrick Jenkin, turned the appeal down. With the Prince of Wales, most of the Conservative city fathers and, rumour has it, the Prime Minister all against the idea, who is a mere Secretary of State passing through a department on the way to the House of Lords to think otherwise? So, the long-dead German architect and his design could finally be laid to rest. What did happen to the £250,000 model?

Despite his erudite rehearsal of the catechism of international modernism, Peter Palumbo clearly has a genuinely Catholic architectural taste, and there is no harm in that. Anyone who collects houses as a hobby has a very special place at the architectural table. He believes, quite simply, that there is room for everybody. He has even commissioned Quinlan Terry to embellish the landscape of his English home with a 90 foot folly of a tower.

Amongst others, Palumbo is the proud owner of three of the most important houses of the 20th century. At the top of the list, the Farnsworth house, which he agreed to purchase in 1968 the year before Mies died. He has had to completely refurbish the property inside and out as the original owner Doctor Edith Farnsworth, who took over the building from the architect in 1951, had let it go to wrack and ruin. She may not have understood the majestic intentions of the Miesian design, but the historian James Marston Fitch certainly did: 'To acclaim Mies for the monumental purity of his forms and yet deplore their malfunction in some pragmatic details is rather like praising the sea for being blue while chiding it for being salty, or admiring the tiger for the beauty of his coat while urging him to become a vegetarian'. Palumbo admits to spending no more than a week a year in the Farnsworth.

Then comes the house by Frank Lloyd Wright in Pennsylvania, six miles from Fallingwater and one and a half hours south of Pittsburg. It is a little known mountain house of 1954 designed by Wright at the age of 87, five years before his death. Palumbo fits in an occasional family visit on his way, for the third house in the collection: Le Corbusier's Maisons Jaoul, built in the same year as the Frank Lloyd Wright house in the Paris suburb of Neuilly-sur-Seine, just west of Paris. The brick and reinforced concrete house has undergone extensive restoration so, along with the Farnsworth, collecting Modern Movement masterpieces is an expensive business. It also sets out the huge breadth of architectural taste – from the steel, glass and travertine marble of Chicago to the exposed shuttermarked Breton brew of Corb at his most uncompromising, via the twilight subtlety of Frank Lloyd Wright at the end of his life.

If we are to understand Palumbo's next move at the City, the variety of styles of these houses gives us a hint; as does his reaction to the hypothetical offer of a further house for the collection. He would commission Frank Gehry,

Ludwig Mies van der Rohe, The Mansion House Square scheme

whom he considers the most 'outstanding architect in America today'. What would the house be like? That would be up to Gehry. From Gehry to Mies, Corb to Wright, a collection of this breadth and distinction is either the acquisitive ambition of genuine Catholic architectural taste or the indecisive hoardings of no particular taste at all. The rich and famous, through the very extent and magnitude of their wealth, may need excusing from the directions of personal preference which influence the rest of us. With only two penny pieces to rub together, any stylistic or artistic decision of patronage or preference is important. If there is only enough in the old cigar box to buy just one limited edition print to speak of personality and preference then the decision could be life defining. If there is unlimited dosh to fork out then maybe we would all end up like the Baron von Thyssen in the Villa Favorita on the banks of Lake Lugano, surrounding ourselves with a self-satisfied collection that did nothing more than speak of our wealth rather than our discernment, inclination or artistic judgement.

Well, for sure, Peter Palumbo surprised most of us with the choice of his second architect back in 1985 when he reluctantly accepted that Mies could finally be allowed to rest in peace. In characteristic and applaudable fighting mood, on receipt of Patrick Jenkin's unfavourable decision he asserted that he would live to fight another day and that he would name a new architect for the site within a month. I wonder where he was when he pondered the choice of national and international significance. A decision of architectural patronage which would ricochet around the world and undoubtedly stir up the British planning system yet again in a thoroughly healthy way? Was he sitting in Farnsworth on one of those five blissful days? Maybe on the outskirts of Paris enjoying the final restoration of Corb's Catalan vaults? Or near Pennsylvania, dreaming of the Gehry house? He may just have been 'at home' as *Who's Who* has it at Bagnor Manor, near Newbury in Berkshire. One way or another with whatever influence you care to pick out of the basket of choice, he chose the late Sir James Stirling, who had recently shocked the architectural cognoscenti by rejecting modernism as dead, mumbling veiled confessions over the indiscretions of brutalism and lording the virtues of a newly emerging English brand of Venturian Post-Modernism.

Quite how Palumbo could reconcile the shift from Miesian international modernism to Stirling's brand of semiotic ramblings of Post-Modernism, it is hard to understand. On the surface the explanation seems contradictory: 'Mies' architecture was an architecture of contrast, Jim Stirling's building is a building of context'. Well one thing is for sure, the site hadn't changed so why change the fundamental parameters of architectural patronage. A sign of the times? A shrewd move to attempt to solicit more favourable public reaction through a more contextual building? Maybe a very distinguished and esoteric understanding of the drift of the architectural debate. As Palumbo himself puts it 'Jim's roots were in Classicism and, like Mies, he is an artist; he has a tremendous feel for proportion and space. He understands materials.' Furthermore, he is not a Post-Modernist but rather, in Palumbo's words, 'a founding member of the post-international style'.

'Big Jim' produced an entirely different scheme from that of Mies. A highly contextual building. A mere 95 foot high, filling all of the footprint of the existing site and confronting Mansion House Square with a pepper pot tower with two extraordinary wings. Explain those away – and he did.

Palumbo must have believed that this building would do the trick. Secure the planning consent and finally allow

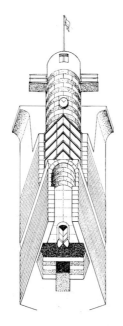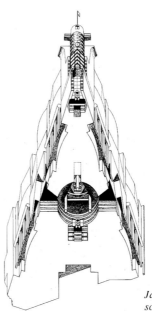

James Stirling, Number One Poultry scheme

God save the Prince of Wales and God save us from his opinions on Architecture

him to consummate his lifetime's dedication to this single act of architectural patronage.

If one battle had been lost it was clear that another had to be joined. A battle of no less intensity, with as many adversaries and urban guerillas waiting in the wings despite his obviously careful choice of, as he saw it, a more sympathetic, caring and subtle architectural solution. One year after Patrick Jenkin had consigned the Mies van der Rohe scheme to the scrap heap, Palumbo lodged the new application for a £60 million scheme which promptly solicited approbation from Lord St John of Fawsley, the Chairman of the Royal Fine Arts Commission, Rod Hackney then president of the RIBA and most of the great and the good on the architectural scene. Except, that is, our Right Royal critic who was bouncing along with yet another strapline coined by goodness only knows whom. Having added his inestimable weight behind the reactionary thrust against the Mies scheme, HRH dealt a devastating blow against Stirling's new scheme likening it to a 1930's wireless set. Quite how Stirling felt about this reference we will never know. But I, for one, rather like Art Deco radio sets: And one thing's for sure, I have little time for architectural criticism which is based simply and only on vacuous but catchy metaphor. Palumbo's reaction, 'God save the Prince of Wales and God save us from his opinions on architecture.' This second chapter in the Mansion House saga is shorter but as complex as the first. Several designs by Stirling. Endless discussions and debate with the City of London Planning Officers and then the inevitable long and highly expensive public inquiry.

The Secretary of State appointed Mr BD Bagot as the inspector for the inquiry. Not a name that conjures up a great deal. Apparently he is an architect, but it takes a certain brand to opt to spend their professional lives sitting at the high bench in judgement over planning decisions. Bagot heard endless eloquent and often verbose evidence on the virtues of the Stirling scheme. To the then Secretary of State, Nicholas Ridley, he affirmed that 'everybody accepted that the existing buildings were of both individual and group value, and not to be demolished save in favour of an outstanding replacement.' He went on to say that a new building on the site would provide a 'vital opportunity' for 'a considered, mature work by a British architect of international stature, of whose achievements the nation can be justly proud'. And, at a stroke concluded that Stirling's building 'might just be a masterpiece'.

Ridley, who as Lutyens' grandson kept his own aesthetic preference to himself, accepted Bagot's recommendations with alacrity. Maybe he knew he was shortly to lose his place on the cabinet or maybe he simply wanted to show the Government's disquiet with the reactionary views of the Prince of Wales and his dabbling in legal matters in an unconstitutional way. After all, a Prince with a mid-life crisis should hardly be allowed to upset both the National Gallery extension proposals and an acknowledged Tory supporter's ambitions for the heart of the City of London. No sooner had Ridley endorsed Bagot's recommendations and approved the scheme than Palumbo was forced to take up cudgels yet again, and unexpectedly, against the charity Save Britain's Heritage, whose president is Mr Marcus Binney, now architectural correspondent of *The Times*. SAVE took Ridley, that is to say the Government through the office of Secretary of State, to the Court of Appeal on the basis that the decision in the planning appeal did not give sufficient reasons for the decision in favour of Palumbo.

By a fascinating twist of English law the case before the three appeal court judges, now adjudicating between SAVE and the Secretary of State, now Governor of Hong Kong, Chris Patten, did not allow the owner and promoter of the site, Palumbo himself, a say in the proceedings. SAVE, it would appear on the surface, had no argument with Palumbo himself. He was just there to provide the battle-ground and foot most of the bills. The heritage fogies were fighting their battle against an errant Government who had had the courage, for once, to support private architectural patronage and who were, thanks to Ridley, prepared to take an enormous risk in the belief that great architecture could result.

Unbelievably, SAVE won their case in the appeal court on 30 March 1990. The judges ruled that Mr Ridley had failed to give adequate reasons for his 'radical departure' from Government policy which said that the demolition of listed buildings should not be allowed unless every effort had been made to preserve them. So there. All that for nothing. Yet again, and SAVE were awarded costs estimated at £80-90,000.

So that was that. On no – it wasn't by a long chalk. It was surely patently unreasonable for a good English subject to lose his rights to develop land in his ownership as a result of a court case between two third parties in which our subject had no say. SAVE may have won their battle against the Government in line with English law but, somehow, the whole thing lacked common sense and equity. I wrote to *The Times* in support of Palumbo in May 1990:

> The Court of Appeal recently quashed the decision letter of June 8 1989, from the then Secretary of State for the Environment, Nicholas Ridley, permitting the James Stirling design to be built on Number One Poultry. It did so because of the failure of the Secretary of State 'to give proper reasons for his decision'. This casts doubt on the reliability of decision letters granted by the Secretary of State and is therefore of concern to

architects as well as planners and developers. This is especially so as the court did not specify the sort of detail that a Secretary of State would in future be expected to give in considering whether or not to permit demolition of listed buildings. It is to be hoped that the House of Lords, whose permission I understand is being sought for an appeal against the decision of the Court of Appeal, will clarify the position with a definitive judgment.

That seems to sum it up. Poor old Peter should at least be allowed the last say. And, I am happy to say, their Lordships agreed. And then, having agreed to an appeal, against the appeal their Lordships were to learn that they were soon to be joined by Mr Palumbo, who was given a Life Baronetcy by Margaret Thatcher in her resignation Honours List. Coincidence? Chance? An irrelevance? Certainly a twist worthy of any lightweight novel by Jeffrey Archer. Perhaps the truth is more prosaic – a mastery of administrative law and the sort of fierce impartiality for which the Law Lords are famed. And then, on 30th April 1991 victory at last appeared to be within our Peter's grasp, his new colleagues in the Lords gave that final approval. The Lords in support of His Lordship Palumbo of Walbrook awarded costs against SAVE, this time estimated at over £100,000.

A year later Palumbo is still battling on against the bureaucracy of the City. As his office so elegantly puts it: 'The road closure order has been applied for and published by the Department of Transport. The City of London is claiming rights to the sub-soil under a Statute of Charles I in 1638 and have not conceded that they have no rights. We are seeking a Declaration from the Chancery Division of the High Court to determine who is the rightful owner'.

Following James Stirling's death on 25 June 1992, I, for one, am prepared to give Palumbo, The House of Lords, Mr Bagot, Jim Stirling's partner Michael Wilford, the benefit of the doubt. I would certainly much rather have any intelligent new building (even a post-international style building) on the site at Number One, Poultry, than the decaying group of Victorian mediocrity which has stood, for so long, in the way of one man's single-minded, dedicated pursuit of the highest level of architectural patronage. I would rather have had the Mies building by far, and along with it a new Square for the City. But as that is not to be, may we please be presented with the Stirling design, regrettably posthumously, before more dust gathers on 50 times God knows how many rooms full of filing cabinets in some woebegone office in the City of London which stand as solemn, painful and expensive reminders of the ludicrous costs of the British planning system when it is consistently abused, misused and manipulated as a passive device to avoid the necessary activity of change.

Palumbo sits in quiet elegance in his office at the Arts Council of Great Britain just off Smith Square in Westminster. A stone's throw from the residences of half a dozen or more Cabinet Ministers and, on a quiet evening, within earshot of the Orchestra of St John's Smith Square. The Arts Council building has been declared a no-smoking zone. Palumbo graciously offers his guests the best Havana cigars in the world. The terrace outside his quiet eyrie, designed by Tess Jarray who has made the most magnificent job of the new piazza outside the Symphony Hall in Birmingham, has one of the most stunning views of the rooftops of the Palace of Westminster Abbey. His desk here, like others around the world is immaculately furnished with 'natural objects, pens and objects from antiquity'. Nothing is left to chance, everything is as tailored and considered as his suits, shirts and shoes. The Lord Palumbo of Walbroook is the most influential figure in the Arts in the 1990s. The Secretary of State for Heritage may appear to hold the purse strings (although he is only a conduit from the Treasury to the Arts Council) but Palumbo sits on the bridge with a clear view to the artistic horizon of the millennium and beyond.

So, has Peter Palumbo earned the right to the title 'Lord Arts'? His single-minded pursuit of Mansion House Square alone, would have done it. Maybe his unique collection of houses, with the cost of their restoration and upkeep, would have done it as well. Or, for that matter, his huge personal collection of art. Or even his gift of a Henry Moore altar to St Stephen's Walbrook. One way or another the life and times of Lord Peter are woven into the fabric of post-war British arts culture. As for architectural patronage no single figure comes near him. He is head and shoulders above the rest. Without a stick or stone of a building to show for it he is this country's most prominent private architectural patron. He is all too often called a Renaissance Man; likened to the Medicis with the predictable and sinister overtones of the influence of Machiavelli. These comparisons could not be further from the truth. Everything in Palumbo's life is publicly transparent. We even know the address of his house in Paris. Were he to be buried, like the youthful Prince Tutankhamun, with his most precious belongings, he would take a good bottle of wine, probably 1929; a picture by Andy Warhol who 'captures the icons of our age so beautifully'; an architectural drawing by Mies or Frank Lloyd Wright; or maybe even a Piranesi. That about sums up the man. Elegance, culture, artistic, good taste and a single-minded, some would say obsessional, dedication to the art of architecture – or at least one project. He would do well to remember now that 'Big Jim' is laid to rest, that the postman sometimes only rings twice.

One man's single-minded, dedicated pursuit of the highest level of architectural patronage

XV

A PLURALIST ALTERNATIVE
SUHA ÖZKAN

As with so many other disciplines, the architectural profession has undergone dramatic changes over the past 20 years. Inevitable and unalterable transformations have required all those involved with architecture to re-define the profession, its scope as well as its discourse, and to accommodate any number of new and unexpected situations, some of them of an urgent nature. The validity and effectiveness of the profession were put under harsh scrutiny, as discourse seemed eventually to reveal increasing uncertainty and ever-penetrating probity: 'What', was always asked, 'is architecture, and what is the proper role of an architect?' In response, new concepts and new terms emerged, as architects assumed the roles of 'agents of change', 'social advocates', 'enablers', and 'decision-makers' in addition to their more poetic place in the field of fine arts, as designers, artists and sculptors of form. Architecture itself, as Sir Nikolaus Pevsner postulated, lay between a bicycle shed and a cathedral, and the definition of architecture began to accommodate simultaneously a wide range of alternatives.

This new sense of questioning was not, however, shared by all, and a small elite continued to fashion prestigious – and often exquisite – commissions which were lavishly published in glossy journals; alas, these noble artefacts, like the expensive journals, had little impact on or relevance to the vast majority. The rampant growth of the built environment had surpassed professional architects; much lay in the hands of mercantile developers, but the largest part fell to the individuals, communities, and societies. Those lacking most in means and abilities, were also most in need, and thus undertook the provisioning of their own environments in whatever fashion possible, whether legal or not, reflecting their own needs, aspirations, and tastes. This was nowhere more evident, as it is today and promises to be tomorrow, than in the Third World.

During the recent past, it is the urban environments that have suffered most tragically, although the rural areas have not escaped ravage and disintegration. The irreversible process of change has rapidly altered the natural as well as the built environment, and predictions for the future warn that this disfigurement will continue at an alarming rate.

Meanwhile, the architectural elite continue their weighty discourse and seek to re-instil meaning and significance into an architecture which they feel has been robbed by the so-called Modern Movement. The debate is highly charged, heavily rhetorical, and strongly laced with finely-tuned semantics. In the meantime, the cries of hundreds of millions remain unheard, and can have but little hope in an architectural profession seemingly enchanted only with itself. It never deigns to see, the plight of decaying cities, inadequate services, and the homeless many.

Still, the lonely voices of the concerned few pointed to the resources of traditional processes and patterns which had, in the past, resulted in suitable, if not always perfect, built environments, usually endowed with authentic cultural richness, and often attaining harmony and beauty. The role of individuals and societies in determining their own environment, loudly voiced by Turner, helped foster the concept of 'appropriate technology' which depended upon people themselves and the recognition that their own participation was the only available resource on which they could truly rely. That resource continues to be a formidable one.

Once again, the architectural elite turned a deaf ear, and relegated such concepts to a realm of anthropology, leaving others to worry about urban and rural shelters, or cultural heritage.

Nevertheless, a few flames of hope illuminated the wilderness. Hassan Fathy had begun the valiant call for an architecture for the poor. Charles Correa sought an architecture sensitive to the climate with his slogan 'form follows climate'. He implicitly nurtured the legacy of Jane Drew and Maxwell Fry who had tried to adapt the grand strategies of Le Corbusier to the realities of India and to implement their own ideas in Africa. In London, Otto Koenigsberger remained dedicated to the training of 'alternative' architects capable of encouraging environmentally sensitive architecture and of coping with the emerging realities of the urban dilemma. André Ravereau and Roland Simounet began serious efforts in the Maghreb, and Geoffrey Bawa undertook a similar self-committed mission in the lush tropics of Ceylon. In Turkey, Sedad Eldem sought a modern identity for the traditional Turkish house, and in Bangladesh, Muzharul Islam concentrated on developing an architectural expression reliant upon limited resources and affordable technol-

Tilework inside an arcade in the Mausoleum of Sidi Sahib

Kairouan Rehabilitation Programme, Kairouan, Tunisia

Opposite: Abdelhalim Ibrahim Abdelhalim, Cultural Park for Children, Cairo, Egypt

ogy. Rifat Chadirji in Baghdad strove to develop a culturally rich architectural idiom of his own. And in concert, many of those concerned came together under such leaders as Doxiadis and the Ekistics Center in order to attempt a re-formulation of urban planning.

For the most part, the Western media and profession remained sceptical at best, and ignorant of these pioneers and the emerging consciousness that had produced them. It was not until the 1970s that public awareness in the West began to awaken to the need for environmental protection and to focus on the imperatives of human rights. Around this time, the notion of a 'master plan', as a sort of heaven-sent panacea, began to give way as people themselves became active advocates for and participants in the shaping of their own environments.

It was in the midst of this confused state of affairs that the Aga Khan took the initiative to actively encourage the built environment and architecture of Muslims. With a small group of architects, thinkers, and scholars, he elaborated an award committed to exploring architecture in Muslim societies and to identifying worthy examples there that merit encouragement and demonstrate to others possible solutions and approaches which might be applied elsewhere. Thorough and meticulous procedures were put into place for the documentation and evaluation of building projects, and a series of seminar meetings was organised on a regular basis in order to enhance and nurture the learning process. The seminar topics were widely varied, from housing to symbolism, from architectural education to the architecture of public places, and focused on urban centres as well as the rural habitat. At each meeting, international participants joined local architects, planners, and others to share ideas and establish dialogue. Site visits were organised as an important component of every meeting, and provided first-hand testimony of the actual conditions at every seminar locale. The chosen venues where the seminars were organised demonstrated the wide variety of cultures, climates, and geographies of the Muslim world: from Central Java to Andalusia, from North Africa to China, from Cairo to Malta, to Sana'a, to Dakar, to Istanbul. The published proceedings of every seminar were widely distributed to increase the scope of participation and interest and to provide the widest possible access to the thoughts and ideas.

Four award cycles have been completed since 1978. 12 international and three regional seminars have been held. Over two million dollars have been awarded by the consecutive Master Juries to 48 building projects, and two special awards have honoured the life-long work of Hassan Fathy and Rifat Chadirji. A wealth of material has resulted from the study of candidate buildings and the documentation centre established in Geneva is the most comprehensive and important facility of its kind in the world.

When seen together, the seemingly disparate building projects that have received awards, and the topics of all of the seminars, reveal a number of key issues and focal points that remain at the heart of the Aga Khan Award for Architecture: architectural heritage, cultural identity, environmental and climatic awareness, continuity with the past, reality of the present and contemplation of the future, appropriate technology, and social and environmental harmony.

The very first cycle soundly tested the established programme and procedures, and confirmed the Award's reputation not only as the world's most prestigious, but also as its most determined and serious architectural award. From 1978 to 1980, five international seminars were held in Paris, Istanbul, Jakarta, Fez, and Amman, bringing together the widest possible range of those involved in the shaping of the built environment. As never before, a platform for serious enquiry was opened without the restraints – and without the fear – of governments, politics, and officialdom, yielding a critical debate on issues of the utmost concern. The contributors to the emerging dialogue were a curious mix of architects, technicians, scholars, and everyday people concerned with their environment. They represented a wide spectrum, from little-known and emerging talents to the most celebrated international architects, from East to West and North to South, from modest masons to heads of state, from behavioural scientists to financial planners, and included women as well as men, young and old, and any number of languages, cultures and races. In short, the Award gathered together the rich range of contrasts and variety that constitute contemporary Islamic societies.

Interest continued to be generated, and the media came to be curious about this peculiar new enterprise. By the time the first awards were announced in Lahore in 1980, considerable enthusiasm had been aroused in anticipation of what many expected would be modern-day equivalents of the Taj Mahal or the Alhambra. And, indeed, the awards came as a surprise. There were, to begin with, 15 of them, and, alongside impressive examples of contemporary design trends, figured slum quarters, simple housing, a modest school, stretching from Senegal to Indonesia. The jury citations emphasised the notion of 'search', and proudly presented this disparate group of 15 buildings as notable achievements that contributed to the quest for excellence in the built environment. The conception of the Award as an ongoing process, embracing a panoply of concerns and divergent directions, has become a central tenet of the organisation and, combined with the 'space of

Raif & Ziad Muhanna, stone building system, Dar'a Province, Syria

East Wahdat Upgrading Programme, Amman, Jordan

freedom' created by the seminar forums, the notions of quest and process came to identify the Award above and beyond the recognition of individual buildings and the attribution of the half-million dollar prize fund.

The emphasis placed by the first jury on encouraging community efforts had two important effects: firstly, it served as a source of inspiration, pride, and encouragement for some of the world's poorest communities, by acknowledging their efforts to create their own living environments. Secondly, it brought such efforts to the attention of the architectural profession and the world at large and, most importantly, accorded them a status equal to that of any other example of good architecture. These same motivations would be reinforced by all of the subsequent juries who continued to appreciate and to honour community efforts and commitments to life, family and well-being.

Not only was the upgrading and improvement of poor communities a focus, but the provision of new and appropriate housing has been a constant concern of all Award cycles. On a variety of scales related to meeting the needs of all levels of society, the various housing projects demonstrate a great variety of design approaches in both urban and rural contexts, and the levels of technology employed reflect traditional as well as contemporary standards, usually addressing craftsmanship as well as structural systems, and always emphasising the basic need for shelter, for the poor, the rich, and for all those in between.

Throughout, appropriate technology has been a feature of the premiated buildings and, once again, the vast array of applications testifies to the diversity of societies comprising the Islamic world. Daring and innovative, some of the awards reveal the most sophisticated use of modern technology anywhere in the world. In Jeddah or in Paris, these marvels of invention have demonstrated the Award's concern for progress and the exploration of often pioneering directions for future development. In turn, too, the time-honoured traditions and techniques that have not changed for centuries reveal the application of appropriate technology combined with an inherent respect for the past. The mud mosques in West Africa call on the skills and talents of artisans whose knowledge has been transmitted through generations, to remain as vital today as many centuries ago. Drawing on the skills, resources, and materials at hand, these talented efforts use traditional techniques, improving on them slowly and economically, often helping to train new craftsmen in the process, and making new techniques and applications available to others to replicate and modify as conditions require and resources permit.

Reinterpretation of past approaches to design, construction, and technology, as well as tradi-

tional functions and programmes to contemporary contexts, embody many other winning projects. These, too, have been vehicles to further enhance traditional skills or to express traditional forms in new styles. Contextualism, at both urban and rural scales, has been an important way of establishing continuity with the past while contributing to the rapid advances of 20th-century life. Inspiration is drawn from the full breadth of the architectural heritage of Islam and from the specific styles and forms that developed uniquely in diverse historic societies.

Care and concern for the splendid legacy of past eras are evident in every cycle of the Awards, and the restoration and conservation of monuments and historic areas has drawn wide attention. The encouragement of traditional skills and crafts, often in danger of disappearing, is an important component of these projects. The economic revitalisation of historic areas has been of special note, as has the use of some buildings for new functions. These awards have helped show that, with sensitivity and care, historic monuments and areas can once again become vital and dynamic components of contemporary society, blending the past with the present.

And yet, the Award has not been able to address several areas of great importance. Industrial facilities, transportation networks, and major infrastructural efforts are conspicuously absent amongst the winning projects, even though they are increasingly evident in environments throughout the world. Weakly represented too are health facilities, landscaping efforts and open public spaces, although a notable project in Saudi Arabia demonstrated the potential for using natural elements with sensitivity and success in the landscaping of a desert setting for an important new development.

Since its inception, the Award has sought to address the manifold and complex factors contributing to today's architecture. The geographic span of winning projects, the multiplicity of building types, and the range of societal issues addressed have yielded a pluralism much wider and much richer than has previously been encompassed in the domain of architecture. The danger of permitting this sense of pluralism to deteriorate into complaisance has been avoided by the creative and well-considered structuring which reinforces the relevance and validity of each of its component parts. The sense of critical debate and the efforts of committed individuals working earnestly together to achieve a common goal have helped ensure a sense of purpose and meaning. With integrity and, at times, audacity, the Award has attempted to discover and to understand contemporary architecture in Islamic societies and has hopefully contributed to the larger effort of encouraging its enhancement and, thereby, the lives of many.

Yousef B Mangunwijaya, Kamping Kali Cho-de, Yoyakarta, Indonesia, detail

Yousef B Mangunwijaya, Kamping Kali Cho-de, Yoyakarta, Indonesia, courtyard

An extract taken from Architecture for a Changing World *Academy Editions, London, 1992*

FREE SPIRIT
IN ARCHITECTURE
O M N I B U S   V O L U M E

Edited by
A Papadakis
G Broadbent and M Toy

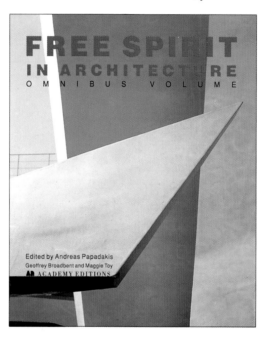

There is a new spirit in world architecture, set fair to make the run-up to the millennium the most exciting era since the birth of the Modern Movement. The *Zeitgeist* is one of renewal, excitement and freedom, with innovative architects moving from the realm of artistic and academic theory to the building site, realising projects expressive of a full release from previous style restrictions. And never before has the creative drive in the field found such multifarious expression; no single school or movement can be said to dominate, in terms either of construction or design. As Andreas Papadakis and Kenneth Powell write: 'The figures whose work is collected together here are the liberators, the architectural resistance movement. They are fighters for freedom, but this does not make them anarchists in the usual pejorative sense. Like all the best anarchists they have a definite, positive sense of the way things should be, but they value freedom more than rules and believe that a little confusion and annoyance is preferable to unquestioning obedience to discredited authority.'

Free Spirit in Architecture presents a visually rich and textually authoritative overview of the works in question, with a number of specially commissioned articles supplementing a selection of material previously published in issues of *Architectural Design.* Architects featured include many of the world's most illustrious, such as Peter Eisenman, Itsuko Hasegawa, Daniel Libeskind, Wolf Prix, Bernard Tschumi and Lebbeus Woods, while an introductory essay by Professor Geoffrey Broadbent provides a clear analysis of recent theoretical and built work.

264 pages, over 300 illustrations mostly in colour, and many line drawings
ISBN: 1 85490 129 X Hardback £39.50; ISBN: 1 85490 130 3 Paperback £27.50

ACADEMY EDITIONS • LONDON
42 Leinster Gardens, London W2 3AN Tel: 071 402 2141

BOOKS RECEIVED:

CLOISTER DESIGN AND MONASTIC REFORM IN TOULOUSE: The Romanesque Sculpture of La Daurade *by Kathryn Horste, Clarendon Press, Oxford, 1992, 389pp, b/w ills, HB £80.00*

BUILDING CONSTRUCTION AND DESIGN *by James Ambrose, Van Nostrand Reinhold, New York, 1992, 403pp, b/w ills, PB £34.00*

GOOD ENOUGH IS NOT ENOUGH: Observations on Public Design, *by Per Mollerup, Danish Design Centre, 1992, 115pp, colour ills, HB price N/A*

CITY CHANGES: Architecture in the City of London 1985-1995, *edited by Richard Burdett, Corporation of London and The Architectural Foundation, London, 1992, 63pp, b/w ills, PB price N/A*

TOWARDS AN ECO-CITY: Calming the Traffic *by David Engwicht: Enviro book, Oxford, 1992, 192pp, b/w ills, PB £9.99*

INTERIOR DESIGN MANAGEMENT: A Handbook for Owners and Managers by Christine Powtrowski, Van Nostrand Reinhold, London, 1992, 338pp, HB £32.50

ENERGY CONSCIOUS DESIGN: A Primer for Architects *edited by John R Goulding, J Owen Lewis and Theo C Steemers, Batsford, London,1992, 135pp, colour ills, PB £25.00*

THE BEST IN OFFICE INTERIOR DESIGN, *consultant editor Alan Philips, Batsford, 1992, 224pp, colour ills, HB £35.00*

THE ARCHITECTURE OF EUROPE: The Ancient Classical And Byzantine World 3000 BC-AD 1453 *by Doreen Yarwood, Batsford, London,1992, 166pp, b/w ills, PB £15.99*

ARCHITECTURE AS ANOTHER NATURE *by Itsuko Hasegawa, Columbia University, New York, 1991, 23pp, PB price N/A*

EPIC SPACE: Toward the Roots of Western Architecture by Anthony C Antoniades, Van Nostrand Reinhold, New York, 1992, 298pp, b/w ills, HB £29.00
In this comprehensive work Anthony C Antoniades views the evolution of spatial concepts and architectural forms through the epic writings of Indo-European and European cultures. He propounds the idea that each epic represents a crystallised statement of the culture and civilisation that generated it and contains the earliest examples of human architecture.

THE CITY ASSEMBLED: The Elements of Urban Form Through History by Spiro Kostof, Thames and Hudson, London, 1992, 320pp, b/w and colour ills, HB £28.00
This independent study follows the evolution of the city's components, and traces the story to the present day, showing how the issues remain fresh and engage with our own day, often in unexpected ways. This is an exercise in architectural and social history and a case study for the present. Urban form is never innocent of social content: it is merely the matrix within which we organise daily life.

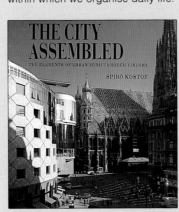

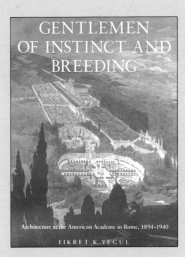

GENTLEMEN OF INSTINCT AND BREEDING: Architecture at the American Academy in Rome 1894-1940 by Fikret K Yegül, Oxford University Press, Oxford, 1992, 242pp, b/w ills, HB £40.00
This is the first historical and critical overview of the education received by Fellows at the prestigious American Academy in Rome during the period from its foundation in 1894 to the Second World War. Fikret Yegül shows the growing tensions within the Academy between the reconciliation of excellence in historically determined aesthetic norms and the freedom of artistic expression and choice. Using source material and architectural drawings he shows how the Academy resisted change until after the Second World War when it began to recognise new trends in art and architecture.

THE GOTHIC CATHEDRAL by Christopher Wilson, Thames and Hudson, London,1992, 304pp, b/w ills, PB £12.95
Christopher Wilson has approached the deeply researched subject of Gothic architecture from a new angle, firstly focusing on the interaction between design and the requirements of the patrons and secondly, putting himself in the position of the masons who built the great cathedrals. Alongside this Wilson discusses chronology, structural techniques and stylistic developments. For his tremendous achievement he was awarded the Alice Davis Hitchcock Medallion by the Society of Architectural Historians of Great Britain for an outstanding contribution to architectural history.

THE NEW FINNISH ARCHITECTURE by Scott Poole, introduction by Colin St John Wilson, Rizzoli, New York, 1992, 224pp, b/w and colour ills, HB price N/A
This volume is a rich, detailed and long overdue examination of Finland's vital contribution to 20th-century modern architecture over the past four decades, particularly the work of architects who continue to wrestle with the lessons of modernism and the legacy of Aalto. 13 architects and firms are examined individually in well illustrated chapters. Amongst others, Monark, the student collective that won the national competition for the Finnish pavilion at the 1992 World's Fair in Seville is featured. Two essays by Scott Poole provide an historical overview of Modern architecture in Finland, defining the work of Alvar Aalto and the work of the rationalist school that followed him in the 1950s including Aulis Blomstedt, Aarno Ruusuvuori and Juhani Pallasmaa.

NATIONAL STYLE AND NATION-STATE: Design in Poland from the Vernacular Revival to the International Style by David Crowley, Manchester University Press, 1992, 149pp, b/w ills, HB £29.95
The complex debates surrounding Polish design are examined by addressing issues concerning the visual representation of national identities. Crawley argues that the emergence of the Polish national consciousness was unique and distinct from those of dominant European states and that artists and designers played a central role in maintaining a vital central Polish culture in its turbulent political history.

Andreas Papadakis

presents

THEORY+EXPERIMENTATION
AN INTELLECTUAL EXTRAVAGANZA

A collection of the most stimulating and varied architectural work in the world today highlighting the major theoretical preoccupations of architects working in the 90s, this volume explores the interplay between theory and experimentation revealing how both are integral to architectural practice.

Theory + Experimentation is not only a source book of an international array of architects and ideas, an intellectual extravaganza of architectural theory and its realisation, but also contains extensive biographies of 35 architects. It is the result of the events at London's Royal Academy of Arts and the Royal Institute of British Architects and includes Bernard Tschumi's 'Six Concepts in Contemporary Architecture', published here for the first time, and a forum discussion of architects, academics and critics. Essays by Daniel Libeskind, Thom Mayne and Lebbeus Woods throw into debate the state and direction of architecture today. Unique to this volume are many pages especially designed by the architects themselves, giving the practitioners the opportunity to present their three-dimensional architectural ideas in two-dimensional book form.

Theory + Experimentation includes extensive presentations of some of the recent key international projects that have been influential in architectural schools and landmarks in the history of contemporary architecture. Above all, it reflects the position of architecture now – as Bernard Tschumi states: 'to "define" a space . . . physically and conceptually, is exactly the place where architecture is.'

420 pages, over 850 illustrations, mostly in colour
ISBN: 1 85490 157 5 Hardback £49.50

ACADEMY EDITIONS • LONDON
42 Leinster Gardens, London W2 3AN Tel: 071 402 2141

STONEHENGE TOMORROW *by Peter Lloyd Jones and Theo Crosby, Kingston University and The Royal College of Art, 1992, 56pp, b/w ills, PB £6.00*

URBAN DESIGN: Street and Square *by Cliff Moughtin, Butterworth Heinemann, 1992, 224pp, b/w ills, HB £29.50*

THE RED CROSS MUSEUM: Architectural Notes *by Pierre Zoelly, Birkhäuser Verlag, 63pp, b/w ills, HB price N/A*

AESTHETICS OF BUILT FORM *by Alan Holgate, Oxford University Press, Oxford, 1992, 289pp, b/w ills, HB £40.00*

THE ARCHITECTURE OF EUROPE: The Middle Ages 650-1550 *by Doreen Yarwood, Batsford, 1992, 201pp, b/w ills, PB £15.99*

ALVARO SIZA *by Brigitte Fleck, Birkhäuser Verlag, 1992, 143pp, b/w and colour ills, PB price N/A*

NORMAN FOSTER *by Daniel Trieber, Birkhäuser Verlag, 1992, 143pp, b/w and colour ills, PB price N/A*

BALINT NAGY BALINT *preface by Arpad Mezee, Exhibition House of the Budapest Gallery, 1992, 64pp, b/w and colour ills, PB price N/A*

NEW SECOND CHAMBER OF PARLIAMENT BUILDING *by Government Buildings 010, CIP Koninklijke Bibliotheek, The Hague, 80pp, b/w and colour ills, price N/A*

FEATURES, APPLICATIONS AND MANAGEMENT *by Peter F Jones, Macmillan Press, Hants, 1992, 340pp, PB £40.00*

BUILDING ECONOMICS FOR ARCHITECTS *by Thorbjoern Mann, V Nostrand Reinhold, New York, 1992, 190pp, HB £29.00*

DESIGN DRAWING TECHNIQUES FOR ARCHITECTS, GRAPHIC DESIGNERS AND ARTISTS *by Tom Porter and Sue Goodman, Butterworth Heinemann, Oxford, 1992, 144pp, b/w ills, PB £14.95*

THE NEW DESIGN SOURCE BOOK: A Visual Reference to Design from 1850 to the Present Day by Penny Sparke, Anne Stone, Emma Dent Coad, Felice Hodges and Hugh Aldersey-Williams, Little Brown and Company, London, 1992, 224pp, colour ills, HB £19.99
An updated revision of an established classic, this comprehensive reference book delves into the economical, technological and social elements which have affected design from the Arts and Crafts Movement of the mid-19th century to the present day. Written with great clarity, it is an essential purchase for anyone interested in the history of design and the influences which have moulded its development.

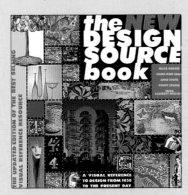

A HISTORY OF OTTOMAN ARCHITECTURE by Godfrey Goodwin, Thames and Hudson, London, 1992 (Reprint), 511pp, b/w ills, PB £19.95
This book traces the development and influences of Ottoman architecture in a very thorough and succinct manner, placing an emphasis on the independent historical style which it reserves in the course of art and architectural history; an element which is not always fully appreciated by the general public. The text is accompanied by maps and numerous pictures.

FANTASTIC FORM: Architecture and Planning Today by Bill Risebero, Herbert Press, 1992, 192pp, b/w ills, HB £14.95
A topical and controversial book in which Bill Risebero examines what has followed the eclipse of modernism. Set in a wide context the architectural theory and practice of the last decade is evaluated and the implications for the future assessed.

STRATEGIES IN ARCHITECTURAL THINKING Edited by John Whiteman, Jeffrey Kipnis and Richard Burdett, MIT Press, 1992, 256pp, b/w ills, HB N/A
The essayists in this volume raise the notion that the once supposed autonomy of architecture is an illusion; at best a suspect quality, at worst a mask on a series of transactions and false stabilities that architecture ensures in a culture. The writers depict certain operations of power by aiming the line of a text against it or threading it through the architecture.

THE WRIGHT STYLE: The Interiors of Frank Lloyd Wright by Carla Lind, Thames and Hudson, London, 1992, 224pp, colour ills, HB £25.00
In this book Carla Lind explores the creations of Frank Lloyd Wright from the origins of his style to more than 40 of his houses. Wright was concerned that his houses should be built as musical symphonies, where all the parts come together to create a unified, harmonious whole and in all cases he himself designed the basic shell as well as all the interior decorative works from furniture and carpets to murals and light fixtures. Lind does full justice to Wright's creations with a book which is rich in details, facts and accompanying pictures.

GEORGIAN LONDON by John Summerson, Pimlico, 1992, 328pp, col ills, PB £15.00
The story of Georgian London as it really was, a product of ambition, industry and sometimes genius. Statesmen, connoisseurs, merchants, visionaries, architects and jerry-builders are among the many characters who people this remarkable history of London at the height of its glory.

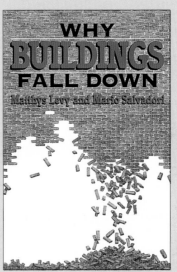

WHY BUILDINGS FALL DOWN by Matthys Levy and Mario Salvadori, WW Norton & Co, London, 1992, b/w ills, HB £17.95
Even the seven wonders of the world, which it must have seemed would stand for ever, have all but one, fallen down. Buildings have fallen throughout history whether made of wood, steel, reinforced concrete or stone, but these failures do respect the laws of physics. All are the result of static load or dynamic forces, earthquakes, temperature changes, uneven settlements of the soil, or other unforeseen forces. A few are even due to natural phenomena that engineers and scientists are still unable to explain or predict. The stories in this book are very human ones, tales of interaction of people and nature, of architects, engineers, builders, materials and natural forces; all coming together in sometimes dramatic and always instructive ways in the places where we live and work.

THEORY & EXPERIMENTATION

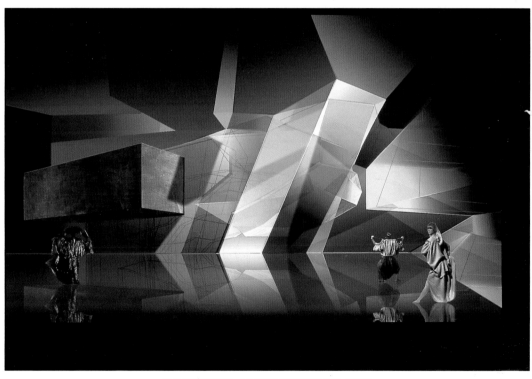

BAHRAM SHIRDEL, NARA CONVENTION HALL, JAPAN

Architectural Design

Edited by Andreas C Papadakis

THEORY & EXPERIMENTATION
ARCHITECTURAL IDEAS FOR TODAY AND TOMMORROW

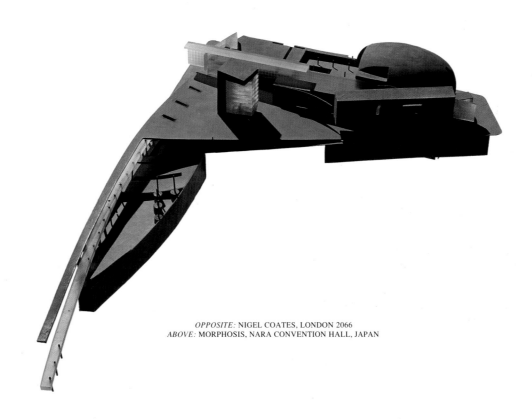

OPPOSITE: NIGEL COATES, LONDON 2066
ABOVE: MORPHOSIS, NARA CONVENTION HALL, JAPAN

ACADEMY EDITIONS • LONDON

Acknowledgements

The concept of this magazine has its origins in a series of discussions with numerous architects and critics, especially Bernard Tschumi, Peter Eisenman and Daniel Libeskind, culminating in the Theory + Experimentation Intellectual Extravaganza, a series of events made possible with the unique collaboration of the Royal Academy of Arts, the Royal Institute of British Architects and Whiteleys and with the support of over 30 international architects, numerous critics and many other educators and students.
We are grateful to Sir Roger de Grey, President of the Royal Academy of Arts, for his encouragement and support, and to MaryAnne Stevens who jointly organised the Annual Academy Architecture Lecture and the Academy Forum at the Royal Academy; to Professor Robert Maxwell, for coming at such short notice from Princeton to chair the Academy Forum; to Sir Philip Dowson; to the President of the RIBA, Richard McCormac, and his staff, particularly Constance Barrett and Kate Trant; to Mark Watt, Director of Standard Life Assurance, owners of Whiteleys, and to Sian Fisher, their Exhibitions Manager. We would also like to thank the many participants of the Forum and Symposium for responding promptly with enthusiasm and for allowing us to reproduce their contributions in this issue

All material is courtesy of the architects unless otherwise stated

pp46-53 We are grateful to Bernard Schneider of the Berlin Stadtforum for providing us with the video tapes of the Berlin City Forum and also to all the participants

pp73-96 We would like to thank Bartomeu Marí of the Fondation Pour L'Architecture, Belgium, for his assistance in compiling this section and to Jonathan Wood of Branson Coates Architecture for his persistence and enthusiasm

Photographic Credits
pp8-41, Mario Bettella; pp54-57, Susan Swider; pp70-73, Botond Bognar; pp73-96 Stephen White, E Valentine Hames, Carlo Gianni and Nishi Azabu

EDITOR
Dr Andreas C Papadakis

CONSULTANTS: Catherine Cooke, Terry Farrell, Kenneth Frampton, Charles Jencks
Heinrich Klotz, Leon Krier, Robert Maxwell, Demetri Porphyrios, Kenneth Powell, Colin Rowe, Derek Walker
EDITORIAL TEAM: Maggie Toy (House Editor), Nicola Hodges, Iona Spens
DESIGN TEAM: Andrea Bettella (Senior Designer), Mario Bettella, Jason Rigby
SUBSCRIPTIONS MANAGER: Mira Joka BUSINESS MANAGER: Sheila de Vallée

First published in Great Britain in 1992 by *Architectural Design* an imprint of the
ACADEMY GROUP LTD, 42 LEINSTER GARDENS, LONDON W2 3AN
A MEMBER OF THE VCH PUBLISHING GROUP
ISBN: 1-85490-138-9 (UK)

Contents

COOP HIMMELBLAU, ZKM KARLSRUHE

ARCHITECTURAL DESIGN PROFILE No 100

THEORY & EXPERIMENTATION

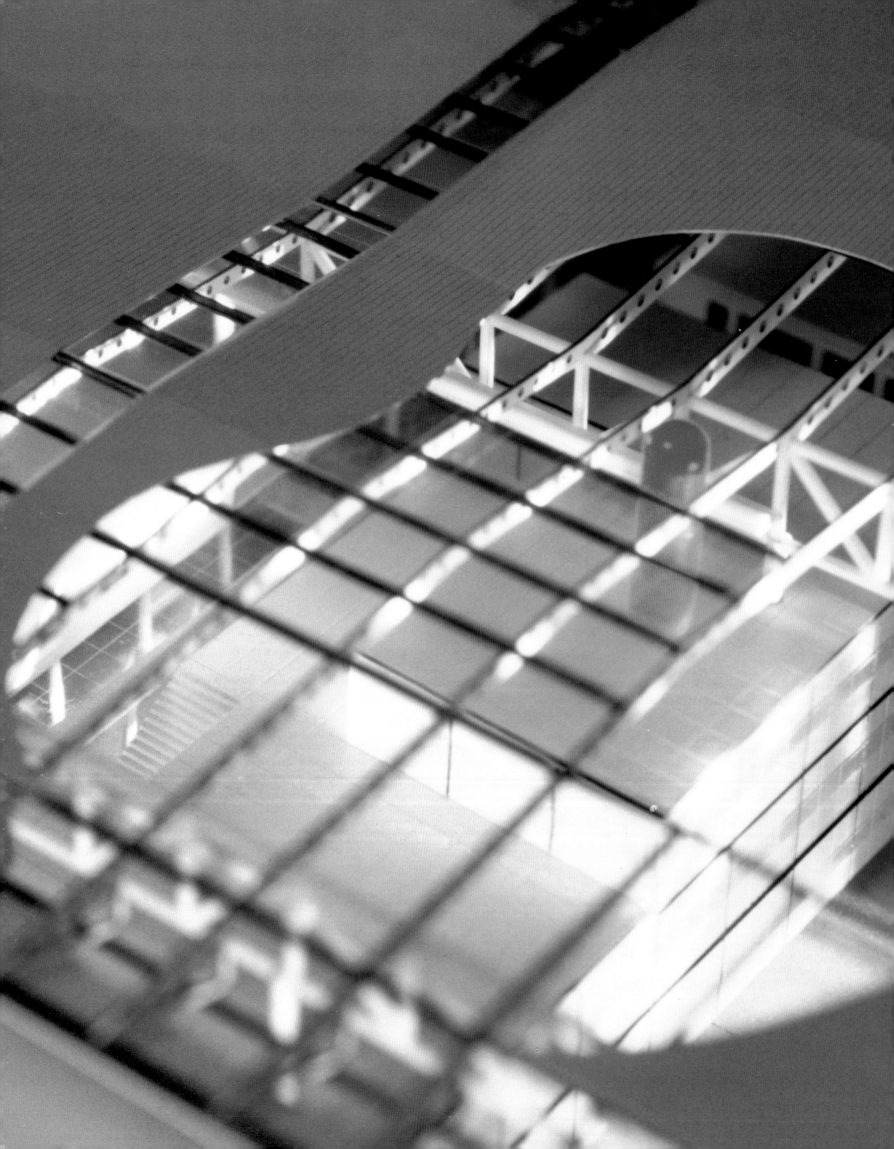

AN OCCASION FOR CELEBRATION
ANDREAS PAPADAKIS & KENNETH POWELL

The 100th issue of a magazine is bound to be an occasion for celebration. Under its present editor, *Architectural Design* might be said to have achieved a certain maturity. But maturity can bring complacency and self-satisfaction. The theme of this 100th issue of *AD* is intended as a clear message that the magazine will continue to do what it has done in the previous 99 issues: to provide a forum for the discussion of radical and innovative ideas in world architecture. *AD* has consistently championed the belief that theoretical discussion is an essential part of the wide debate about architecture and that a purely practical or empirical view of the art of architecture is inadequate.

In this issue, *AD* presents a cross-section of the work of some of the most innovative architects on the international scene who combine extensive practice with a commitment to the development of a viable theory of modern architecture. Many of those whose work is presented have featured in our pages on a number of occasions, from their early days onwards. It is with some pride that we acclaim them as the leaders of a new wave of thought and experimentation. All are theorists by definition, but none believes that theory in architecture can stand apart from practice nor that the art of building can be detached from the context of cultural, economic and political life.

Daniel Libeskind, for example, believes that architecture is a 'wholly political' art. 'Pure' theory is, for Libeskind, the theory of unreality. His project for the Potsdamer Platz in Berlin challenges accepted, hierarchic images of the city (which have been enshrined in the officially favoured masterplan for this crucial quarter of the city). Libeskind's Jewish Museum, which is moving towards construction, is powerfully symbolic on a number of levels, aiming to unsettle and disturb the spectator, to make him, perhaps, a participant in the dramatic story it tells.

The weekend of exhibitions, lectures and discussions arranged by Academy around the theme of 'Theory and Experimentation' in the summer of 1992 addressed the dilemma facing architects today, at a time when they can no longer ignore massive political, social and environmental issues affecting the world. The architect is forced to take a stance. Libeskind has responded boldly to the challenge as has Itsuko Hasegawa, working in the very specific context of contemporary Japan. Hasegawa expresses her fears about the future of a mechanistic, product-dominated society. Her humane, highly expressive, inclusive, diverse architecture is a commentary on the modern Japanese city. As is the work of Bernard Tschumi on the typical Western metropolis. Tschumi can be presented as a destructive influence, embracing disorder and dissonance. Equally, however, his penetrating analysis of the nature of the modern city is the prelude to an attempt to make sense of the irrational. His current work on urban masterplanning, following on from his famous plan for Parc La Villette in Paris, is essentially humane *because* it makes provision for the variety, disjunction and irrationality of human life. How many Modernist

visions have foundered on the dogged illogicality of mankind?

Tschumi is essentially a compassionate influence: he rejects the prescriptive orthodoxies of the Modern Movement. At the same time, he gives modern architecture a new impetus. Tschumi's work, and that of Peter Eisenman, rehabilitates the art of architecture as a positive force in the world, capable of educating and communicating. Eisenman's Wexner Center is one of the icons of the new architecture of the late 20th century, remarkable for its rejection of old certainties and old values. Eisenman is a figure especially associated with the interest in Deconstruction which shook the architectural world a few years ago. Widely seen then as a new 'movement', it has since emerged more clearly as just one strand in the new theory of architecture, a way of thinking and analysing, not an all-embracing philosophy. Deconstruction has achieved its task – of cutting a way through the old architectural logic – and can now be seen as a positive influence, not (as some critics have alleged) a theory of negativity.

Deconstruction played an especially important part in the erosion of old 'functionalist' theories of architecture. But the new architecture has not discarded the modernist's social vision. The 'public domain' of the client for the new experimental architects today, who see architecture as much more than a form of self-expression, a species of large-scale gallery art. Sometimes their proposals are almost too radical for their patrons. Lebbeus Woods' view of the modern urban condition is anything but reassuring. Wolf Prix of Coop Himmelblau has spoken of the 'ivory tower of theory' and of the duty of architects to fight on the streets with their buildings. Günter Behnisch wants an architecture which 'empowers the weak'. Ted Krueger and Ken Kaplan reject the 'one choice society' of the present day and call on architects to strive for a society where there are real choices, genuine freedom. Le Corbusier spoke of the choice facing society in the inter-war years: architecture *or* revolution. The new generation of experimental architects believe that architecture means revolution.

In this stimulating, ever-changing scene, the British architect Nigel Coates occupies a special place. A constant experimenter and innovator, whose talents have found particular expression in a stunning run of interiors, Pop Baroque, coffee bar kitsch and Deconstructivist themes run wildly through his work. But there is another Coates, a radical urban thinker, who wants to break down old, hard-edged views of the city – essentially the ancient view of the city as a heavenly ideal, the City of God – in favour of a new vision of the city floating, changing, a realm of experiences, processes, interactions. Anti-utopian and humanistic, Coates has produced a view of London which challenges all the old certainties and is really about giving back the city to the people. His work typifies the new architecture of theory and experiment. It communicates, it intrigues, it questions and, in the end, it demands a revolution in the way we live.

Opposite: Bernard Tschumi, Le Fresnoy, School of Arts, France

ACADEMY FORUM
THEORY & EXPERIMENTATION

ACADEMY INTERNATIONAL FORUM: The Royal Academy of Arts, , London. Saturday 13th June. The International Forum on Theory & Experimentation in Architecture.

ROBERT MAXWELL: I am personally very grateful to Andreas Papadakis who presents this intellectual extravaganza for bringing the general austerity of British culture into the modern times, and I welcome you in his name.

We are here, Bernard and I, to be co-chairmen. I am here because I talk like an Irish man – rather easily – and don't mind what I say. Bernard thinks very carefully about what he says because it has to conform to his built work, and so we will play this game together and we will try to keep in touch with each other. Before we come to the first speaker, however, I would like to open the question as to what is theory. I would like to ask if there is anybody here who could pick up from the idea of theory that we had ten years ago; Stan Anderson's basic theme was that if you know how to contain sand it is a pretty good material to build on. That was the scientific idea of theory. Daniel Libeskind, would you like to tell us what theory is?

DANIEL LIBESKIND: Well I am glad to have been asked by Professor Maxwell what theory is, but the question already puts us back into another millennium, doesn't it? About the year 1,000 they had a lot of conferences like this all over Europe. They discussed the problem of demonology, nihilism and what was happening to the world. We know from history that that was an incredibly crucial period, because around then we had a kind of beginning of the Renaissance; later it was called the 12th-century Renaissance and later still, what we understand to be the beginning of science.

I don't know why, but theory has changed its role relevant to building, just as ideology changes roles vis à vis politics, and therefore we might expand the notion of theory to include political issues that concern building. I think that the radicality of architecture is that it is wholly political and cannot take place outside a political context, whereas writing, literature, music and art can find a place in, let's say, a subdued political context. And what is political about architecture is its realisation. What we have here is the possibility that the oppressive limits that have been placed on who is an architect and who is allowed to practise and who is allowed to speak, have opened up politically. Of course it is not so difficult for a poet – it might be difficult to publish, but one could continue writing; a composer's works might not be performed, but it is possible to write, it's the political radicality of the act that is limited. To get a building built is a political act of enormous proportions. Not only does it involve the public at large, but it also requires substantial environmental resources, not only in a financial sense, but spiritually as well. I believe that we have entered into a radically political time, meaning that architecture which is beyond theorisation, which has not come out of any linear process of anticipation and expectation, is being realised. Therefore, if we are talking about theory, I would not limit it to the scientific theory that you referred to – the theory of science, the theory of physics – but

Daniel Libeskind, Potsdamer Platz

would include political theory. That brings us to the first sentence of Aristotle's *Metaphysics*, which I have always been amazed by. It says 'all men desire to know,' which is a blatant lie. I don't know how Aristotle and the whole Greek tradition was able to get away with such an incredibly unempirical statement that no one ever challenged. And theory, from the very beginning, developed on this flawed foundation which assumes a kind of universal desire that is simply not verified by our experience. This premise is based on the fact that there were three people in Athens who wanted to know, who then extended the idea to the entire world and universe and all time and juxtaposed this with the humility and vulnerability of a world in which almost no one wants to know. That is what I call Theory and Experimentation.

What is the emblem we could put onto Theory and Experimentation today; where would one find one? I thought that we had one, but it's in the zoo. The zoo emblem that I would propose for Theory and Experimentation and for architecture and for city developments today is the emblem of the horned animals. Well I thought about horns; the hardening into something fantastic. They are the one part of the animal that survives, out survives, that is permanent and inorganic.

LEBBEUS WOODS: I wonder if there has been in recent memory a real theory of architecture. What theory is supposed to do is set up a framework where you can predict what will happen under certain conditions in the future; that is the main purpose of theory in science. The experimentalist then gets to work to spin out a series of events that somehow firmly attempted to be predictive. It seems to me that this idea of desire is very strong; architects, shall we say, adopt ideas to suit their purpose, but this is not exactly theory. So I would challenge whether there has been any theory, although there have been methods of theorising.

ERIC OWEN MOSS: Maybe the problem of the idea of 'theory' is that it was supposed to be generic, meaning it applies to everybody. And if there is a theory which is useful for us, it is an anti-theory, which means that everyone has his or her own private theory. And by the way, Aristotle was not necessarily wrong when he said 'everyone wants to know'; that is not a complete sentence. To know what? If the 'what' is private, then maybe he is right.

DANIEL LIBESKIND: It can't be true in Aristotle's context because in Greek a private individual is an idiot.

ERIC OWEN MOSS: That may be true.

L to R: Bernard Tschumi, Eric Owen Moss, Daniel Libeskind

ROBERT MAXWELL: What do you mean true? Wittgenstein spent a lot of time on the private language theory. If your theory is private, this corresponds to architectural students worldwide now when they tell us the basis of their design. 'I decided to have a wall here,' they say, 'this wall is meant to be both a barrier and a link, thereby cancelling out the logical meaning of the wall.' And all the grey-bearded members get into problems. The 'privately' defined theory is an excellent eurhythmic for the designer, but surely when we are talking about theory we are talking about something that is *shared*. The scientific theory that has lasted since Francis Bacon was one where knowledge was supposed to be cumulative, amounting to a kind of peak in the Hegelian sense and leading to final enlightenment, but you could always add *on*, and this was to do with the fact that if you discovered cold fusion in your laboratory, it didn't work unless the other guy could discover cold fusion in his laboratory, and if he couldn't then it wasn't effective theory. There is something we have to respect in science even though technology, which we thought was an aid to better living, turns out now to be a kind of ogre that is eating the world. One has to say that if man took power from God effectively, the instrument of doing that was the assumption that through science the truth could be verified and established. So we have to respect that side of science and we are not claiming to have such a theory of architecture. When I spoke on this in 1979, I insisted that there were two theories of architecture, the scientific one, which deals with about ten per cent of the useful info, and the other one, which is entirely cultural, which is shifting, which moves along, and of which we can never be certain. That is the theory we are talking about today. Does anybody finally want to bring up scientific theory and not put it to bed?

KEN KAPLAN: I find a problem with the programmatic description of putting theory in front of experimentation. It seems to me that the way scientists work is that first they experiment then, at some point, they form a hypothesis; they develop procedures and methods and then if after a number of years they finally come up with a theory which they agree on, they immediately have a conference and decide they are going to try a new method. The idea of putting theory in front of experimentation seems to me backwards. What is interesting and relevant to architects is to be able to experiment. That is the word I find least understood – well, least applied – in architecture.

BERNARD TSCHUMI: A minute ago Robert Maxwell mentioned the cultural aspect of theory, which Ken Kaplan touched upon, when he said that experimentation should precede theory instead of the other way round. I'll tell you a little story. Anthropologists used to be very irritated with Lévi-Strauss because he had stayed all his life in a small room in Paris developing a theory, and only went into the field to check it. I don't think that this is a chicken and egg situation. What is interesting, however, is that theory has always existed in architecture but it has taken different forms: from Vitruvius to Durand to Le Corbusier to a variety of people today. But it has always had a relationship to the culture and the science of its time. Durand's architectural theory is directly related to developments in science, positivism and so on. So what is happening today? I think that perhaps with Vitruvius, Durand and Le Corbusier the aim of architectural theory was to get closer to the centre of architecture, whereas nowadays the aim is to understand the margin of architecture, the areas that need experimentation. To get back to your point, architecture is very much a form of knowledge like any other, like mathematics, physics, literature, and to expand that form of knowledge for those who are interested in those limits you obviously have to look at the margins, at experimentation or the purely analytical, theoretical approach; again I don't make a hierarchy and a chronology of precedence between the two. This becomes a fundamental notion, but it also implies that the definition of architecture has changed, that maybe the definition is at the margin and not at the centre any more.

BOTOND BOGNAR: Traditional disciplines are breaking down and architecture has expanded tremendously. Indeed I agree with Bernard that it is not the centre but the periphery. The mechanical world is breaking down and the world is virtual reality and simulation and imagination or illusion . . .

ROBERT MAXWELL: Yes, one shouldn't forget though that technology is the offspring of science, it is not a separate force. Technology has only developed in the West because of the discoveries of science. So when we refer to technology, we are referring to the last point of application of science in the Western sense.

ERIC OWEN MOSS: What you are saying is interesting. I mean you may be saying in the end that this kind of scientific positivism is something one could use; that technology is additive and cumulative, implying a kind of progress, that things improve. One theory surpasses another theory, knowledge increases. For example, there is a Babylonian map which goes back about 4,000 years which is essentially an attempt to map the sky in order to map the earth. Like in the caves of Altamira, this map tries to explain what is up 'there' in order to feel that one can explain and make intelligible what is down 'here'. This reveals the basic need to predict and to prognosticate and the need to understand that there's a kind of continuum, predictability, future. It is an anti-nihilistic approach.

So what Robert Maxwell may be saying is that it's not true that when you pick up something new, you give up something old and that the idea of science is a virtue and its child a stepchild. Now technology is under suspicion because science is under suspicion, and the idea of progress and that things get better and improve, is under suspicion. What are all the pieces that we have come to know and associate with the act of building? Is it possible, in recognising them as what they were, to redefine them and make them something that they were not, so they have both their old identity and a new identity as well. In a recent building in LA the vertical wooden doors evoke the image of a table top while the actual table surface is made out of steel doors. Now nobody can be sure.

THOM MAYNE: Modernist theories of the expanding universe, which are completely connected to the three

L to R: Lebbeus Woods, Robert Maxwell, Thom Mayne

essential notions of time, progress and forward direction, are channelled into the most fundamental operative fact that we can discuss and anticipate, that of reverse change, which totally challenges the whole notion of time and memory and so on and so forth.

CONRAD JAMESON:There is something sad about the avant-garde in modern architecture. It is not just that it is a Johnny-come-lately when compared to the more advanced arts like music, painting and literary criticism. Even more embarrassing is that it is a Johnny-come-sweetly. It will say much the same as do the other avant-gardes, but is heavily sugared.

The habit of over-sweetening in an architectural avant-garde goes back in time. Compare the approach of painting and architecture when both took up Cubism, one before the First World War, the other after it. For Picasso there was a risk of disorder, a danger of slipping into solipsism of the kind you can see in his series based on Velasquez's *Las Meninas*. No object has its own identity as all identity is in flux; the hues of dull grey evoke a nightmare. But when Le Corbusier and Amedee Ozenfant took up Cubism they turned it into what they called Purism. Out goes the risk. In comes a stable order of universal geometrical forms, indeed a stripped down revival of classical architecture. The whole system of Purist thought is reassuring in a series of interlocking definitions: the functional is the geometrical and the geometrical is the universal and the universal derives from human proportions.

Now we have only to put such self-explanations against the Post structuralist writings of Paul de Man or Jacques Derrida to realise that all we are tasting is sugar. The 'confused, disorderly city' isn't ratified because people like and dislike, but by agreeing and disagreeing in the light of the forum.

Eisenman's sense of presentness is simply a cop out. Derrida's point is that presentness is a self-pleasing ruse. There can be no raw perception, as perception is itself like King Midas, who transforms the world even in trying to touch it. Our very language, argues Derrida, structures and conceptualises. What Eisenman is playing back isn't post-modernism, but the sentimentality left over from the Romantic movement whereby the artist's own subjectivity was an authority unto itself and the artist becomes Shelley's unacknowledged lawgiver of the world.

BERNARD TSCHUMI: Wait a second. I actually quite object to what you just said. It may appear to be so, in that purism is a sweetened version of Cubism or Deconstructivism or whatever you call it, a sweeter version of this or that. To say that would imply that architecture is involved in the business of translating other theories, whether they come from music or from literature, but architecture has certain things that are absolutely specific to itself; it deals with a certain materiality that the philosopher cannot approach. What-ever the architect writes, experiments or theorises, he or she may be involved with building it, therefore entering a world which is quite different from the one of translation. Suddenly the architect hits something hard, something that resists, and there enters a new set of conditions which is quite fascinating, because at the same time it can also bring back certain theoretical concepts to the very people who might have inspired him in the first place. In other words we are in front of a process not only of architects importing things from other disciplines – we all do that, it's perfectly normal, scientists also do that from other scien-tists – but also of exporting; this is extremely important, and probably the reason why architecture has become so fascinating for people who are not architects, whether they are writers, scientists or movie makers, is that we are able to touch upon things that help them to go to the next step of their own discipline.

DANIEL LIBESKIND: I understand exactly what you are saying. A Rauschenberg painting is irrelevant in comparison with a building that mimics a Rauschenberg in the public domain. There is a big difference between seeing a painting, a concert, a piece of music, and establishing that act politically, which involves not only the resources of the environment but money and power. I do think that it is relevant to go back to Aristotle, because I would take the idea of knowledge as what can be transformed altogether. We know that Aristotle and the Greeks based everything on their analysis of the organism and of the *thing*, how to craft a thing, and have come to the conclusion that the political statement was defined as a 'well made thing'. But what is valid to contemporary architecture has been building up for hundreds of years. The phenomenon of the Age of Enlightenment is pushing the knowledge of the architect to another extremity where it goes beyond the capacity of the political realm to contain, which means that the model of the organism, the body, the crafted thing has also re-entered politics.

KEVIN RHOWBOTHAM: But to do that the first act is to get rid of what we are now calling theory because what it does is produce a persuasive moment. It is the point at which speculation collapses; it's the thing which drags us back. Let's get rid of theory now, let's kill it here . . . it's already too late probably.

JOHN MELVIN: Do we have to build cosmologies? If I could get back to the political realm, instead of mixing architecture and cosmologies we should actually divide them up, and architecture should explain the world as something that can be understood. Instead of talking about 11 dimensions as scientists now do, perhaps we should return to three dimensions; instead of being dragged down into some black hole of nothingness we should say that the world has meaning.

GEOFFREY BROADBENT: We can't demolish theory because it is there, there is no way you can destroy it, but as you said, it affects about ten per cent of our architecture, and the question is, what about the other 90 per cent? If you talk about the people that are called architectural theorists – you mentioned Vitruvius, Durand and Le Corbusier – they were all prescribers like doctors, so they take maybe 20 per cent of what is going on. What is the rest? I think the rest is philosophy.

BERNARD TSCHUMI: Architects have a tendency to be prescribers. We love to set rules and regulations

Odile Decq & Benoit Cornette, Apple Macintosh Headquarters

that we may transgress. However, since we've been bouncing back and forth on some historical moments, I'd like to pick up someone to act as a moderator. There are two people in the audience who, I think at least for some of us in this generation, were recognised as playing the role of theorists in a way. One is Peter Cook. You wrote a book called *Experimental Architecture* which discusses some interesting things that are being done at the margin. The other one is Hans Hollein, who once wrote 'everything is architecture', which challenged the boundaries of what architecture is. Your statement 'everything is architecture' was in a way the end of architecture.

HANS HOLLEIN: Well, I think it is acceptable that you should have a personal theory. I think any theory, if it is intelligent, can be a very good sort of crutch and a scaffolding to get you somewhere. The Ptolemaic theory of the universe could be used to calculate the ways of the stars perfectly, only it was a wrong theory, as we know; and Copernican theory proved that it was not a geocentric but a heliocentric system, but otherwise this theory worked perfectly; whereas for Columbus the theory that Asia was in the West worked at least to discover America. I think that architects use some of these personal crutches, sometimes intuitively. I also think that many of the things we talk about are more questions than answers, not solutions to a problem but just statements. You don't first analyse the problem and then come up with a solution, just as a painter doesn't have an empty canvas in front of him and say, 'Well, now, what is the problem?'

BERNARD TSCHUMI: What has changed is that now you have university departments, you have chairs in architectural theory. It suddenly becomes a very heavy piece of machinery. Peter Cook was certainly not Professor of Experimental Architecture!

HANS HOLLEIN: Let me just make two points. One is that I made the statement simply to expand the realm of architecture, which has to a large extent come about. You now have virtual architecture, which has never been seen before. I think that flexibility is a realm of architecture, so it becomes a question of definition, of how closely you can define the question of theory.

The other question is that of experimentation; I have big doubts about delegating certain aspects to the realm of experiment. Very often we say, 'this is just an experiment'; in some instances one needs the help of little by-products, but I think it is wrong to delegate every activity which ventures into the unknown to the status of an experiment. We talk this way about Picasso, but it's not a question of *experimental* painting; it was the true belief of the artist who created it, so I am very careful about the question of experimentation.

THOM MAYNE: It seems to me that what you are describing isn't really theory, but a series of ideas that are becoming more and more idiosyncratic and personal, taking with them fragments of notions that become part of a work; whether it is Copernicus, whether it is Einstein or Darwin. We are all more and more aware of ephemerality, of these notions of how the world exists, and the more you are aware of ephemerality, the less you can believe. It affects how you use these ideas because you become hyper-aware of the fact that these ideas are going to be shifting and you couldn't commit yourself to them the way you could two or three centuries ago. But by the nature of what you are saying, they become much more a series of fragmented pieces of ideas and notions versus . . .

ROBERT MAXWELL: The very idea of a fragment implies that you already know what it is a fragment of, or that it is a fragment of something.

ERIC OWEN MOSS: What are you saying, which is, with all due respect, rather Viennese, is a little bit insidious. What it means in the end is that theory, at least on the part of architects, is absolutely disingenuous. What I think, is that there are theories that make ways for moving and doing. It's not really a question of accounting for what is, it is a way of motivating oneself, of moving oneself. It is not in the theory of Ptolemy.

LEBBEUS WOODS: Why are we talking about this guy? He has been dead a long time. Maybe you can come up with someone more recent than Ptolemy.

THOM MAYNE: The point is that there is something there that allows you to operate in the world.

PETER COOK: Something that for me clarifies the whole business, which hasn't been mentioned – and actually probably is a dirty word in these sorts of circles – is that architecture is process. I would like to see that for my own 'core', because I think that all aspects of architecture somewhere along the line lead to building. Even discussion of architecture, even the discussion of the abstract, which might lead to further discussion of the abstract, which might have something to do with architecture, leads to building. And if one calls that a process, to me that is absolutely central to anything one has ever been interested in, which is cause and effect, the relationship of phenomena or things that happen or things that you do or tricks that you play, one leading to the other. It seems to me that theory is those parts of the discussion which one can use without necessarily making reference to the process. I see a red light when the theorising goes on beyond a certain point, when I start to lose sight of its connection to the process.

On the other hand, for me experimentation is very close to the process. Experimentation, as Hans said, doesn't really exist *per se*. It is a sort of greater or lesser degree of what one normally sees connected along a process line. Now I suppose it could be argued, and I find this difficult, that experimentation could be the business of extending theory, but I switch off very rapidly there. There comes a certain point at which if it is not process related then there cannot be experimental theory, there can only be theory. Having listened to this conversation, I am delighted that it has not so far detached itself from architecture. The sooner you can

L to R: Peter Cook, Bahram Shirdel, Hani Rashid

get back to any references to architectural process and to specific pieces of architecture, the better, in order that the theory should have more to say to other theoretical territories than to architecture.

DANIEL LIBESKIND: I am surprised that you say that. I would say that 50 years ago all nuclear technologies in atomic physics were considered totally useless experiments of a theoretical kind. Architects who emulate scientists are the real adventurers because they don't go in like lawyers, doctors and architects to make money and build buildings. They are capable of spending their whole lives with something which might not have any future.

ROBERT MAXWELL: Architects do that too!

GEOFFREY BROADBENT: My interest is in the process of design, which for many years I have seen as a matter of synthesis and evaluation, or in Karl Popper's more memorable words, *Conjectures and Refutations*. That is, having ideas as 'wild and free' as one pleases and then testing them to destruction before putting them into practice. I see this as operating on two levels in architecture: the level of designing an individual building – although few architects 'refute' with the necessary rigour – and the level of whole monuments in architecture of the kind that Thomas Kuhn might describe as 'paradigms'. Of course the Modern movement was such a paradigm, but it has been under fire for the past 20 years or so for failing to deliver the goods. So the more adventurous architects, singly or in groups, have been presenting alternative paradigms: Postmodern Classicism, vernacular, Deconstruction and so on, though they too are subject to heavy refutation. So the 'Theorists and Experimenters' represented here are today's 'conjecturers', which is why I welcome them enthusiastically.

As a design methodologist, of course I am at heart a *functionalist*. I have written many times about the fit of spaces to activities, of the ways in which buildings may – or may not – filter out their hostile climates, about the function of a building as a symbol, its economic implications and its impact on the environment. These for me are the bases for 'refuting' any design; if it survives, then in my view we have a right to build it. This basic sense of fit to human need was damaged and indeed destroyed by much of the Modern movement. Simple, rectilinear, abstract buildings simply could not fit – as Venturi shows – the messiness of human functions. The making of a building to loo*k* like a machine is to take structure and services – rather than use – as the *basis* of architectural expression, and this *by its very nature* interferes with the fit of forms to functions and erodes in the process the very essence of architectural skill, which I take to be the moulding of internal space as walk-in, inside-out expressive sculpture.

It is hardly surprising that our 'New Free Spirits', these 'Theorists and Experimenters', should pursue sculptural forms again – not to mention what Le Corbusier himself called 'the masterly, correct and magnificent play of forms brought together in light'. In pursuit of this at first sight nothing looks more wilful than Frank Gehry's Vitra Museum, yet as one perambulates certain things become clear: that Gehry had a brief – to display chairs as effectively, as dramatically as possible – and that he succeeded by funnelling daylight on to individual chairs, suffusing others with the glow of reflected light and making darkenable rooms where objects could be spotlit. He connected his various surfaces – floors, plinths, and even chair-scale shelving – Corbusier-like, by a 'promenade architecturale' of entrances, ramps, staircases and bridges so the exhibits are viewed from multiple angles. This is why the Vitra Museum is 'functional' architecture of a very high order, in terms of fitting spaces to activities, climatic filtering – especially of daylight – and so on.

Compare this with the Architecture of the British Establishment represented by a building such as Stansted Airport. The urge to 'express' Stansted as a temple to structural expression meant that nothing so vulgar as aeroplanes could be allowed to nuzzle around it. Thus they – and the passengers trying to board them – are relegated to a satellite. Nor are anything so crass as flight-announcement boards allowed to sully the 'purity' of the structure. Such announcements are confined to tiny television monitors which one cannot see for the glare from the curtain-walling, or the high ambient light pouring in from the pyramids which form the ceiling. Of course in any airport, movement must be controlled – in this case by screens located in and around the structural columns, destroying its 'pure' rationale. It is the totalitarian view of people as units to be processed and controlled and of architect indeed as agent of control which, more than anything else, our 'Theorists and Experimenters' seem – thank God – to be challenging. Many of them do this expressively by replacing the military precision of a Stansted with the visual – but by no means functional – chaos of Deconstruction.

Tschumi writes of rejecting such ideas as grand-axial composition, of contextualism, even of 'palimpest', or digging into the site for traces of its previous history. This is why Tschumi used his grid as an 'abstract mediator' between the site and his future design. Tschumi broke through to a level of *public* acceptance that no formal solving of the brief could have achieved. As for Peter Eisenman; he describes his many ways of transcending the brief, or 'deconstructing' it, especially in such projects as Cannaregio West for Venice, Romeo and Juliet for the Venice Biennale of 1985 (lavishly published as Moving Arrows.), the Housing Block for Berlin just south of Checkpoint Charlie, the 'Choral Work' Garden for Tschumi's Parc (more or less with Jacques Derrida) and so on. These show his complex methods of scaling, including 'recursibility' (nesting identical forms within each other at different scales); 'discontinuity' (digging down into the site as 'palimpsest' or quarry as an aid to projecting its future or 'immanence'), and so on.
Zaha Hadid with her Moonsoon Restaurant in Sapporo shows that by using non-conventional forms such as tables like ice-sheets on a lake, ceiling fittings like the belly of a whale, or a peeling orange – she can match human scale with sculpted forms of such quality they might be the envy of any Classicist!

HANI RASHID: If one would actually place theory against experimentation, I suppose our Studio Asymptote, Lise Anne Couture and myself, are probably mostly interested with the problem of experimentation. I

Asymptote, Exhibit at Whiteleys, London

think theory is something that we may sometimes bring to the work, but we discard it as quickly as possible. We get down to work, experiment as feverishly as possible and then perhaps look back at the work, take a look at the theoretical terrain and develop a kind of discourse around that.

The idea that an architect is only deemed credible by virtue of building is something that we are a little bit opposed to. I think experimentation in architecture has the same rights now as art in the early part of the century, when sculptors stopped looking at beautiful form and began doing other things, when painters stopped worrying about the canvas. We probably now stand in a similar sort of unprecedented space.

We have done work loosely based on chaos theory and the attempt to map televised space as a place that actually contains moments of the chaotic that one could unfold from within the cathode ray tube, which has now been sort of demystified into a utilitarian appliance.

We did a series of works done at Columbia University on optigraphs, looking at what we thought was the kind of space that would be revealed when the Berlin Wall was removed. The project began as an optical appliance which could be photographed, filmed video-taped and eventually was us. We consumed the object. I guess it is akin to the process one uses when delving into the computer to create space.

Our way of working doesn't suggest that we are not interested in buildings. We do building proposals as a kind of detour from the experimentation, at the same time, so as not to enforce the experimental work.

We did a series of works done for a conference at the Research Institute of Experimental Architecture on what, at the time, was disinventing gravity space; again there were really glimpses into how to misuse the computer, how to misuse systems, how to misuse rules. Spaces were created as a kind of collapse of the various mechanisms that we were using, ranging from archaic modelling and drawing, to the absolutely novel, that of CAD systems and VBR.

CARSTEN JUEL-CHRISTIANSEN: I want to say something about the question of theory: architects are not usually in the business of building theories and if some of them did it was all normative theory, it was how to do – the Vitruvian, the Palladian, the Bauhaus. We now have so many professors in the theory of architecture; that might be a response to the fact that the object of architecture is disappearing and it needs to be established. It is something that has been going on over a very long period of time; we have had 200 years to become accustomed to living without God as our centre and culture is very slow. Maybe theory is related to both thinking and drawing, establishing architecture both as building and as an object.

L to R: Carsten Juel Christiensen, Wolf Prix, Ted Krueger

WOLF PRIX: That is a good point, that architecture is vanishing and theory is coming up. Even in the Forum title there is no architecture any more: it is 'Theory and Experimentation', but in what? I think that this is the dilemma of the discourse. Theory, in my view, is the explanation of the world. It is a closed system: 1+1=2. And nowadays this has very good connotations. Experimentation is the questioning of the world, ie putting forward concepts which could be a development. And of course 'Experiment' in architecture has a very bad connotation: if you want to insult an architect you say this is only an experiment. I think it is no wonder that there are students escaping into the ivory tower of theory, because architecture nowadays is occupied by architects just building neutral spaces for development. This is the dilemma of the young architects, and I think we should put down theory and get back to experimental architecture's good connotations.

LEBBEUS WOODS: That only works if there is some object theory you can live with. Architects didn't need theory for a long time because they were willing to buy into the prevailing theories that governed all of society. Today if one is willing to accept all of the premises operating in the development of cities, you don't need theory because it's been given to you. But if you say I can't accept all of these assumptions or I don't want to operate within them, you are obliged to develop your own theory.

THOM MAYNE: I was curious that nobody responded when Hani Rashid mentioned Chaos Theory. I would say that there is no developed theory of Chaos beyond the young men at Berkeley who are working with analogue computers and have started this idea. I don't think the people who are working with it can define it other than in the vaguest terms, and I am curious to know the departure point for a set of experimentations which would validate or invalidate this set of ideas 'Theory' has a method of investigation, in the sense that Popper would talk about it, as a method of falsifying solutions or testing ideas.

The qualities that give value and meaning to the world, all that is individual, immediate, circumstantial which otherwise would appear to be accidental and meaningless, become the root of the work. I've been interested in the possibility of defining the agreement between man and nature as a system that is in a constant state of change, where transformation becomes the major characteristic; a system which shifts the emphasis from man versus nature to man and nature as a synonymous, coexisting activity.

LA has been my homebase for the last 15 years. It is a complicated place, a collection of infinite urban functions, an information interactive society; its continuous change makes it incomprehensible. This metropolis is unstable and dynamic: its identity is continually disappearing in its presence. We observe this city today with both fascination and fear; gone are the conventions of boundary, inside/outside, coherency. It is the first major metropolis in which everyone is in a minority, the place which has no majority in place.

To me that conflictual nature is really the essence of the modern city. The world has been radically realigned in terms of our human interactions. The more generalised notion of context as we've been taught it in universities has always included the conventional notion of local influences, physical conditions, demographics, but also contains the remote influences, the global influences and the electronic environment. The methods by which we formulate our values are defined within this broader framework of context and this is an extremely important aspect the approach to the general problem of context as well as one of language in response to this. Associations with our neighbours are no longer based on common interests within the physical geographic domains of the conventional neighbourhood, but within this global condition.

One of the consequences of this breakdown of a conventional notion of community is the loss of the

Dagmar Richter, Exhibit at the Royal Institute of British Architects

21

cohesive concept of the public role, accompanied by a continued advancement of the private persona, as is characteristic of architecture today. The nature of these series of private world views that make up our pluralistic world is in my mind one of the major issues.One of the possibilities that grows out of this condition is an architecture that oscillates between these two poles, maximising their conflictual status.

Modern urbanism has provided the world with a vast legacy of diminished expectations. If architecture has a single mission it is to clarify its intentions and to realign its purposes in the hope of a complex, integrated, contradictory and meaningful co-existence.

CHARLES JENCKS: The population of Greater Los Angeles consists of 12 million people. Encompassing 132 other cities within its bounds, the city grew from its 1781 foundations as a pueblo, formed by a hetero-geneous group of different kinds of people. Heterogeneity has always been there as the site was home to the Gabrielino Indians for 5000 years previous to 1781. Over 200 years the roads and other systems intended to unify Los Angeles, have become more and more various until its heterogeneity exceeds that of New York City, Chicago and San Franciso – the other great centres where they pride themselves on having a radical mixture. LA is a truck culture and a car culture in which all types of people - and of course heterogenisis is all about difference - personalise their houses or cars. It is a culture without a tradition of culture, enabling people to do their own thing on a huge scale.

My basic argument is that heteroarchitecture has a deep reason for being in the city and I've divided up various architects into representational heteroarchitecture and analogous heteroarchitecture. It's really the analogous heteroarchitecture which understands its spirit generally and tries to represent its heterogneity by analogy. As for the more representational ones -'No 2 Rodeo Drive' reveals an attempt, like Disneyland, to reconstruct the heterogeneity of a nineteenth century urban village right next to the existing Rodeo Drive. Therefore it's a kind of double representation of heterogeneity, in other words its mimicking both the nineteenth century street and Rodeo Drive right next to itself. The problem of course, is its literalness and its lack of a kind of self-understanding.

The work of Venturi, when he comes to LA, indicates a self- conscious dealing with this difference and variety. He is one of the few architects who does the representational heteroarchitecture on a convincing level. However, its the others I want to talk about – the analogous heteroarchitects.

It's interesting how far and how deep this new tradition goes. There are twenty or thirty architects who are

Itsuko Hasegawa, I project 1991

practising and you can see many common aspects amongst them. One is that they're rehabilitating existing warehouse buildings using of course very everyday common materials in a way that suggests the building is unfinished, or forever unfinished, or is scaffolding. The convention goes inside the warehouse to treat the existing structure of the trusses and lighting and heating equipment members as part of the new architecture - allowed to exist. The fact that there are twenty or thirty architects doing these kinds of conversions, the fact that they are all warehouses, the fact that they're using materials in a certain way builds up what I would call a recognisable school.

The sensibility of heteroarchitecture has been conventionalised at least since 1977. Gehry started using chain link in a way that showed he was conscious of both its high refinement and its opposite. There are some other obvious antecedents to the sensibility. One is the general movement of ad hocism which came, before the sixties, very strongly within the counter-culture and which of course has always existed. To that, sensibility was part of a general Post-Modern sensibility. On one level of course Venturi formalised' Complexity and Contradiction' but it was much wider and came out of the counter-culture. It was fed into, in the beginnings of Post-Modernism, with work on participation that Lucien Kroll and Ralph Erskine carried through. So that ad hoc sensibility is not unique to LA. It is a sensibility that is shared and dealing with heterogeneity through analogy.

If America is going through a real crisis, a lack of work, and is entertaining itself to death with places like Disneyland, then you find in LA a new building type - a celebration of the office village or the work place as a kind of internalised environment. What I find fascinating about such office buildings is that it is an office village and a much more pleasurable place to spend 40% of your life. in a post-industrial society where office work is in central place and factory work is our leading form of occupation. Everybody is tending to work at home in LA and telecommute, so that these offices have to then make themselves into homes and borrow different building types. This is in a sense the next stage of heteroarchitecture where it conventionalises difference in heterogeneity at the level of building and becomes in effect a small city incorporating in its grammar as much difference as it possibly can.

One fascinating outcome is the inability to distinguish between building type and use and the level of reality that you're looking at. When you go look at this streetscape and see a red mini in the background, a basketball net in the foreground, some protest art of Leon Golo, and the shape known as the 'Gehry Fish', you wonder at what is reality and what is art, what is usable, what is function and what is work. It's one of the really exciting things about this environment is that it completely breaks down the customary distinctions.

Two things, two extraordinary things happen in the office spaces designed by, for example, Moss, Morphosis, Gerhy and Isreal; one is that it cuts through all habitual categories that separate things from each other - that is syntactically, the floor, wall, ceiling, or architecture and sculpture. Secondly, being made out of this material it soaks up all the sound, so if you're there alone you can hear your heart beat or the blood circulate through your veins. These experiences are extraordinary aspects of architecture, comparable to the experience of being alone in the Pantheon beneath its oculus, where the space and the light are an analogue of one's place in the universe. Metaphysics is a major force for opening up our eyes to experiment in architecture, because what cosmologists are telling us today is so extraordinary that it forces a certain kind of change in the language and experience of architecture.

KEVIN RHOWBOTHAM: Just to go back to what Lebbeus Woods was saying, when I say ditch theory it's not to ditch the possibility of speculating about the world in different ways but to be careful of its institutional intention which is to prepare a particular conservative restriction on people who speculate, and we should get rid of it as soon as possible.

ERIC OWEN MOSS: It's not a matter of throwing theory out, but of looking at theories critically and self-critically. For example, Phoebus is one of the Martian moons and it interests me because it is not what it was supposed to have been. In some recent photographs from NASA, it turns out that it rotates the wrong way; it rotates retrograde. It was supposed to have a certain shape, but it doesn't. This is the latest discovery from MIT in Caltec in NASA, and I guarantee that it will finally be replaced by something else. I think *my* hypothesis is that whatever comes together, comes apart and then comes together again in a different way. Whatever the hypothesis is, one knows that the hypothesis will finally be replaced by another hypothesis and then one gets suspicious of all hypotheses. So what do you hang onto? For somebody to say that this is a project without symbolism or to talk about Chaos theory is an absolute oxymoron.

ROBERT MAXWELL: We do have to move on and I personally am suffering from the fact that so far we have only heard male voices, can we hear from the women please.

LISE ANNE COUTURE: I think that a point we keep coming back to – and if you let me speak you'll hear a woman's voice – is this idea of theory somehow answering something, and you say Chaos theory is an oxymoron because you posit that it is going to provide some answers. Maybe the point that we are at in architecture is realising that theory is perhaps most useful for us in just positing more questions.

DAGMAR RICHTER: Robert said something which I found quite interesting, that if theory was the form that contains the sand, then we could build. I find it is actually the other way around; I see sand as the theory or the world view, and if we can give form to the sand then we can build on it. In other words I would like to reverse the relationship between the form and the sand. I don't think we were talking about theory in relationship to architecture. I think architecture is an act of translation or transcription from the non-physical to the physical form, and to bring it back to what Peter Cook said, I think that architecture is not process but initiation of change in a process. Spatial experiments are nothing other than attempts to indicate specific

L to R: Lise Anne Couture, Dagmar Richter, Ken Kaplan

changes in an ongoing process of physical change. Space cannot be timeless; even the definition of space is dependent on time. A great work of architecture cannot be measured by its capacity to be timeless; it cannot be singular but has to be read as a fabric in constant flux. Architectural design has to act as a translator, as an agent between one condition and the one that follows it, which by then is already in a process of change again.

New methodologies have to be found to reflect this reality. As one starts to collect as much physical information as possible, one has to initiate a process of translation, transcription and endless copying of multiple layers of physical, visual and intellectual information into a fabric of working drawings and working models. This will translate the obtained information into the purely physical realm and will be better equipped to reflect the idea of a fabric in constant flux.

In my studio we are experimenting with the gathering of spatial information and the means of producing a set of process drawings and process models through translation, copying and interpretation which could initiate a change in the ongoing process of physical alteration. We use working drawings and models to build further models, which, in turn, employ the previous constructs as a base for a further translation. As the constructs reflect material obtained and therefore describe found space, not created space, the issue of authorship becomes irrelevant. The singular, master author who creates a timeless masterpiece is challenged in the studio's process of production. As every participant in the studio is a translator, she or he permanently has to use different sets of arguments to arrive at formal interpretations of the obtained material. The first set of translations are exchanged between the participants. In the second phase they can choose to interpret each other's constructs. In further developments the different constructs are collapsed together and the outcome can no longer be defined by a specific authorship, but is instead the result of a group's formal collective discourse. This form of authorship as an initiator of a translation in an ongoing process allows us to produce a fabric of spatial possibilities which are then the base for an ongoing editing process where the found fabric supports a construct, which does not necessarily have to look complex, but has to react to the complex and layered nature of the space found.

In my experiments with Century City, Los Angeles, the process was to translate the conditions which we found on skin surfaces and structures into a new proposal. The process drawings we came up with go back into the layerings of physical information. If architecture is a form of translation, what happens if we translate physical form to physical form instead of non-physical form to physical form? And we did some very simple exercises in Century City and translated layers and layers of physical information, investigating the role of the author, the role of the physical information in front of us and how the initiation of change actually works in a design process. It gives us a new notion of architectural space which in itself is not chaotic but which might be a little bit more complex than the belief that object representation might give us one point of view. We were trying to figure out through these processes, with a lot of authors involved, if we could have multiple points of view as a way of producing architecture or initiating change in a physical sense.

We did another project in which we were asked to rebuild Beirut, and we used specific points of view to investigate the mapping of war, the word 'operation' – both in war and in medicine – and used those as methodologies to re-plan the inner city of Beirut. This was for a conceptual exhibition at MIT, and is now in Beirut. The translational act ended in investigating a process where maps and physical information were used to propose a new skin or surface on top of Beirut. This is not what the planners are trying to do right now, which is to destroy Beirut entirely because the ownership is in 3x3-metre parcels and the Souk area is too difficult to deal with. We therefore proposed a new surface on top of Beirut, which would carry air rights, and leave layers in the city so that other initiations could be made. This is a multiple approach to city development. Everyone seems to work in Berlin; we decided that we wanted to translate form into form, so we initiated a studio where we used all the physical information of Berlin to investigate the relationship of vector and physical connections, enclosure and surfaces. We translated physical conditions into other physical conditions, both 3-D to 2-D and 2-D to 3-D.

IAN RITCHIE: One point which people might like to think about is that theory for architecture is in fact a definition of geometric space; it is one of the crucial components of the way we think.

KEN KAPLAN: I disagree that that is what it is exclusively about. What I find most exciting about a lot of the work that I see now is experimentation with the politics of architecture, which I find the most difficult, because it isn't just geometry. Architecture is immensely complicated, especially when you deal with the scale of some of the urban projects. How does one deal radically with politics in those kinds of projects?

DAGMAR RICHTER: I would like to go back to the notion of geometry because we had a long discussion about that a few days ago. I think one has to remember that geometry represents order and order represents politics, and I think there is a very clear line between the three, so if we experiment in geometry we experiment within the realm of three-dimensional order and in the realm of political order as well. When we go back to the public realm, architecture puts theory to form because as the newer theory says, theorists need architects, not architects need philosophers. Theory was once used to create a space of singular reality. Architecture is commonly regarded as a reflection of philosophy and theory, but this relationship has now been challenged by Mark Wigley, who argues that, despite our traditional beliefs that architecture reflects philosophical thought, the system of thinking in philosophy is actually based on spatial and architectural principles. The whole structure of philosophy is architecturally based. Philosophers write in architectural metaphors beyond the linguistic: one refers to the base of an argument, the 'structure' of an argument, an 'ornament'; you can argue for an 'elegant' scientific solution, a 'non-elegant' scientific solution, and so on and so forth. I believe there is a reverse relationship: that philosophy argues architectural not architecture argues philosophical.

BERNARD TSCHUMI: I think we are reaching a very interesting point in the discussion, a moment when form, geometry and politics meet. The point about geometry made me think of one example you all know, the piece of work that Terragni did for the Danteum where he took a piece of literature and translated it into a building, finding a common denominator that was mathematical in the context of a very political regime. Dagmar was talking about the translation of form into form and I think that is exactly the point: where suddenly one realises that architecture has that ability to take a variety of totally incompatible constraints or variables together and play them against one another. Maybe that is one of the definitions of what we are talking about, we deal with the things that cannot be combined with one another and therefore obviously we look for theories.

DANIEL LIBESKIND: I think these are very interesting presentations because they bring to light two things. One is that theory in its very structure is an attempt to globalise and comprehensively understand what is

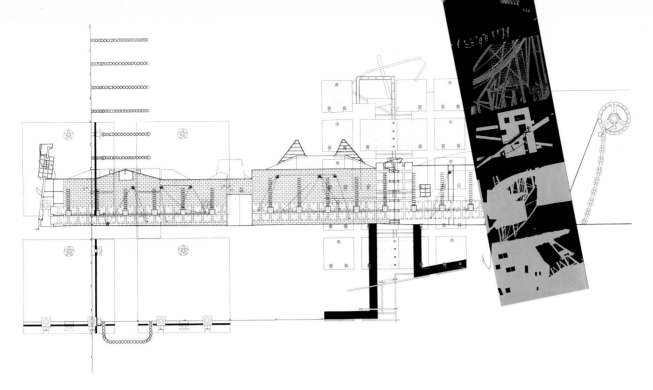

going on, but we are also saying – and I would in this case agree with Eric Moss – that theory even if not *private* is not *one*, and if theory is *many* then it is already flawed and divided from the very beginning. And I think that the definition of geometry, politics and practice as a theory which is fundamentally based on a scientific idea of a oneness of the universe – what Stephen Hawkins is actually trying to do, which is to fulfil, as he says, an eternal dream of mankind, to bring everything to a complete transparency – that is not architecture. Architecture is radical in the sense that it is not modelled today after a scientific theory. It is not modelled after a theory, but is already split heterogeneously; if it was ever one it would have been crushed by the weight of space and politics, yet it continues to exist and be needed.

CONRAD JAMESON: What we are seeing now is a lot of scratching. Theory is scratching. Architects are very upset that they are scratching more and more and they want to stop. People say, 'You won't have this itch if you stop scratching,' but it is not necessarily true; you go on scratching because there is a problem. For a while it looked as though we were breaking up into schools. There was Postmodern with a capital 'P' and postmodernism with a small 'p' and there was high tech, etc, and it looked like each one might at least contemplate something, they would self explain. As time has gone on we now realise that the public forum even for theory itself has collapsed. That's why I find it fascinating hearing about chaos and geometry and this nonsense about architecture creating philosophy upside down. We have lost any public forum at all in which we can talk about city making, politics, morals; these things need a discourse and if that discourse breaks down you will get this kind of conversation.

BERNARD TSCHUMI: I am delighted to have someone to disagree with. Anyone who starts to talk about moral values and the design of cities to me represents something that has been challenged as an ideology. Indeed very much of what is being discussed today is against that discourse of values.

LEBBEUS WOODS: Theory can be tyrannical. I think what we really need is a theory of non-consensus; Deconstruction tried to deal with that in literature. Can you imagine the student saying I put a wall there because I wanted to? The only reason we deplore that is because we form a consensus and say that is not good enough. Why isn't it good enough? What is the basis of your critical judgement? I am fascinated by the

Eric Owen Moss, Nara Convention Hall, Tokyo

idea of a language made up of words that are only used once.

ROBERT MAXWELL: 'TIAOW!' That is a word I'll never issue again. What good does it do?

ERIC OWEN MOSS: Just to support what Lebbeus is saying, if by your somewhat facetious evocation or whatever that noise was, you meant we should get rid of Samuel Beckett, who writes 'blah blah blah', or James Joyce . . .

ROBERT MAXWELL: No, they don't write 'blah blah blah'.

ERIC OWEN MOSS: Among other things they do, because we are debating the merits of this kind of complication.

ROBERT MAXWELL: Well we could go on saying 'blah blah blah' for the rest of the afternoon. The point I'd like to make here is that if you go to literary theory, as Lebbeus has suggested, we don't find that the undecidability of issues has entirely stopped ideas and the theory of literature and philosophy. On the contrary, if we are finally honouring Derrida with a degree at Cambridge University, it is not because he has opened up the world of idiosyncratic utterances, it is because he has renovated a discourse of criticism.

KEVIN RHOWBOTHAM: Nonsense.

ROBERT MAXWELL: He has renovated that discourse by the very act of showing how undecided it is and how it is not based on a final answer; and so to that extent I would say that the new freedom is to allow us to shift around, but still remain people who are born, who are destined for death and who within that brief span have some means of communicating, and death is the control on us, and that means that we can only communicate in a short time and that means that we do actually communicate.

BERNARD TSCHUMI: Theory has to do with definition; architecture has to do with definition. To 'define' a space can mean two things: to define it in the sense of the definition of the word 'space', or to define it in an architectural sense – to put walls around it – and that very double meaning of the word define, define

L to R: Itsuko Hasegawa, Odile Decq, Peter Pran

28

physically and define conceptually, is exactly the place where architecture is.

ITSUKO HASEGAWA: In Japan it is rare to hear the term 'the theory of architecture' repeated again and again. For me theory comes as a result of experiment, and I'm not sure if theory and practice can be discussed separately. My architecture starts from the acceptance of the city, Tokyo. Tokyo retains traces of its origins as an Asian village, while it has grown to a chaotic city fuelled by an enormous economic system and permeated by high technology. Things that should happen only in dreams are turning into reality. Buildings are a straightforward realisation of economical desire. Tokyo is an electronic information society where invisible signals flow, and architecture is a component of an intelligent and emotional city.

Traditional Japanese architecture appears to be dignified, but Nietzsche's 'will to power' is lacking. Architecture in Japan has been a poetic apparatus for experiencing the rich and yet translucent world of human emotions and senses and has been the medium for listening to the mysterious music of cosmos. This is strongly related to the philosophy of Eastern culture in which rational and irrational, general and extreme, can coexist.

We Asian people conceive space as 'basho', which can be translated as 'place' This is related to the fact that most of the performing arts in Asia originally took place outside. The concept of basho/place is integral to human activity from birth to death, and at the same time we know that it reflects the unstable condition of air, light, sound and other environmental factors.

In the field of molecular biology we learn that every living creature uses DNA for its genetic system. Now this knowledge of micro-information systems is being applied to an energy-saving technology through which one common language enables communication among people, nature and science. And here I see the possibility of creating the realm of architecture as second nature, where human nature and scientific technology can coexist.

My architecture is created through a process of filtering my life in Tokyo. Land possesses certain dormant features in the same way as the human body retains a memory of its origin somewhere within it. My objective is to extract those features and let them emerge in the form of architecture. I call this approach 'architecture as second nature'. In other words, to create architecture is to express what one has experienced in life as a human being by using a completely different vocabulary. My approach to architecture is ad hoc rather than an exclusive, formal development. It is not to reject or eliminate diversity but to produce an inclusive architecture that accepts diversity. It is to provide the reality for architecture, not by a logical reason associated with our unified value system, but by a Pop reason based on a diverse system of values. In the sense that it accepts the mysterious nature of human consciousness, my approach might be a shift towards a feminist paradigm.

BERNARD TSCHUMI: One interesting thing that comes out of Itsuko's presentation is that it is part of a cultural reality of practice that is different, I think, from that of many of the people here. Perhaps Odile Decq would like to talk about another cultural reality that starts to question the order Ken Kaplan mentioned what comes first, theory or experimentation.

ODILE DECQ: After the breakdown in the system of architectural education in France architecture was based on a kind of 'bricolage' with the conditions of reality, more than on theoretical experimentation or reflection, and for us theory and experimentation has been experimentation and theory, because of the

Bernard Tschumi
Top L to R: ZKM, Karlsruhe; Kyoto
Station, Japan
Below L to R: Bibliotheque de France,
Paris; International School of
Contemporary Arts, Le Fresnoy

early confrontation with the need for building. Each experimentation, each project has shown us the inadequacy of unitarian systems such as 'modern movement' confronted with the reality of our problems. The modern movement is a great problem in France because it has begun to be a new academicism. The inefficient theoretical systems at our disposal have led us to answer circumstances with relative uncertainty. Confronted with the complexity of our environment we have here built our own system through a series of experiments. The evaluations and criticisms of the results have led us to an attitude of continuous adjustment. For us, to create and conceive is to accept the confrontation with the hazards, to play with these contradictions, to accept and amplify the possibility of ambiguity and to transgress the rules.

BERNARD TSCHUMI: The reason why I suggested that Odile should speak is that most of the people in this room are not the architects who have 20 years of practice behind them but architects who have not yet practised, or are just in the process of turning ten years of intense thinking and experimentation into possible practice, as if the realm of questioning, the realm of theory therefore became the question of a generation. In France it looks as if it is the other way around. They could start building at age 28-29, which is quite different from the Anglo-Saxon countries, and when you've already built 16 buildings you ask yourself the question of theory. But what strikes me is that most of the people dealing at the moment with theoretical issues are one way or another affiliated with universities to the point that it brings a formalisation of it. I get really worried when I see a distinguished Ivy League university advertising for a 'practising theorist', or is it a 'theoretician and practitioner'; so a new category is formalised in the very realm that started with questions.

KEN KAPLAN: I think that is a really good point. My partner, Ted, and I spent a number of years practising something else. He was involved with sociology and I was involved with psychology. One spends most of the time, at least in the field that I work in, thinking about oneself; that's your best tool: your technology is in your own brain and in working with other people. Universities or the academic world may become the only place for things like this, which are rare – for people to sit around and be more crazy than they've been in the office. I find architects tend to be much too unaccepting of their craziness; I think that's what makes a lot of the work I see around here quite mad in a positive sense. I think that it is something that architects seem to be opening up to and I think it's positive.

DANIEL LIBESKIND: I think it is inadequate to make a distinction between the office as a place of conservation and academia as a place where theory is a liberating factor. I think it's actually to the contrary, in my experience, and I think it has to do with what theory is. I would just like to propose a definition, since many people are floating: I would say that theory is a cover-up word, very general, very ambiguous, extremely subtle and flexible. And what does it cover up? It covers up a kind of subversive freedom within various structures, mainly political, which allow the possibility of doing something else. I think in that sense the word theory in architecture would have been defined in another way even 15 or 20 years ago. So theory is a kind of a license, isn't it – going back to Bernard's notion of institutionalising theory – it's a kind of a license under which certain speculative thought can take place even within the university context.

There is that conflict and tension between theory as we know it from the Greco-Roman world, particularly the theories of a detached perspective, immunised from its consequences, or the theory which is radically engaged in the very process of building buildings. And of course it is also a collapse of theory into architecture, a form of revolution, where theory and explanation come after the fact, as if the seats have already been sold in time. The world of events is much greater than all the seats that have been sold. If St Augustine or Socrates or one of the Japanese philosophers came today, where would they be able to practise?.

ROBERT MAXWELL: I really would like at this point to hear a couple of British voices. Like women, the Brits have to be looked after nowadays. I have been used for years to hear British architects say, well that's all a lot of talk, practice is where it really happens. Now it's being said that the only place it really happens is where it is being thought. So the categories are shifting. Perhaps you'd like to start that ball, Peter?

PETER COOK: I think it is very interesting that we have seen a presentation from Japan followed by a presentation from France, and that many of the more distinguished people in the room are transatlantic, but I think that every country believes that it has its predicament, and those of us who work inside academies are of course featured in this because in a sense an academy is a predicament of its own making. As I see it as an outsider, the American predicament is that you have perhaps more than any other country a consciousness of the architect as white-shirted professional; I'll just leave it at that. I mean I think I can understand in a way the great wish on the part of American academies to both distance themselves from that and at the same time serve it; almost to say that whilst you are in this academy we will make you into an intellectual and we will make you able to move the pen faster and so on. And one sees the selfsame guys who were in Cooper Union two years ago sitting in an office down the same street having changed their shirts and dumped their John Hejduk paraphernalia, sadly perhaps, and watching the CAD system . . . I know actual cases of this, and it forces upon them a certain predicament. But on the other hand, when one hits the occasional experimental condition such as a funny old city like Los Angeles – on the occasions when it did building – you do find that the guys teaching are the guys doing some hickory-dickory thing down the same street; and the guys you see in the morning in class are down there planing the wood.

Now the British, our predicament is that we have a very good use of our own language, but by our position as an off-shore island, get rapidly bored with pure ideas. We have tremendous use of the language, and any of us can always sit on an American academy jury and win the conversation game. And yet we have a very different situation in several of the academies, where the most creative minds amongst, let's say, the 30-40-year-olds are teaching: there is almost nothing that you can point to that comes out of the discussions within

L to R: Hans Hollein, Ian Ritchie, Geoffrey Broadbent

that teaching; not that it is not to do with physicality. And of course there is the late lamented AA of the Alvin period, which we all know created a very large number of people who have set a large part of the iconography of the recent period, but at a time when in almost none of them could you find something that was going on down the road. Now that's a very interesting situation. We nonetheless still have the predicament of the English, whose natural manner of survival is to go down to the potting shed and fiddle about with something either physically, theoretically or verbally. You know, we are great fiddlers in ideas. Once you get a sniff of what the theory is, you dismember it; once you get a sniff of how you might hold a structure up, you start to stretch it and pull it; once you get a sniff of the possibility that somebody might do something, you go and destroy it. It was interesting to hear the French predicament, which I have not been aware of. It appeals to me greatly, this fact of being able to do it and perhaps evolve a theory from it or not. Nonetheless, it is interesting to me that where the 30-40-year-olds in France have had the opportunity to build things which we are drooling over, their iconography seems to a large measure to have come from this side of the channel. I always feel that the intriguing thing about Bernard, as somebody who came through the French intellectual system, is that he chose for his formative period to live in this funny city and then to move on.

If I then finish on what I see as the Japanese predicament, it is marvellous that Itsuko Hasegawa has made a presentation, because I have had many funny arguments with my students about her work, which definitely get up the nose of those who wish things to be consequent. They always dismiss it by saying it's too fruity and sweet – they always tend to use the word sweet. It is lovely coming after a remark by Bernard that theory has to do with definition, because I think one of the things about Itsuko Hasegawa's work that gets up the tighter-arsed of my students' noses is that as soon as things start to get defined it undefines them. She is the best of them, but there are a number of other younger Japanese architects who are extraordinary at undoing and moving on, though they are also quite good at being able to assemble some theory which is usually about 1,000 years old. They have this way of being able to say, 'actually, it's to do with the notion of ma.' We unfortunately don't know whether they are having us on or not (I don't think that matters, by the way). We all carry our predicament with us, and what would be the fruitful thing to come out of this afternoon would not be that we arrive at an agreed theory or agreed attitude towards theory. The most important and most interesting people sitting in this room, in my book, are the experimenters anyway.

ROBERT MAXWELL: Well, we have a whole line of people wanting to speak now. Thank you, Peter, you have put the English point of view very vaguely, just as I'd hoped. Max, do you have something to say?

MAXWELL HUTCHINSON: With an English voice again. As an architectural politician and a practitioner, I can take in as much of this theory as you guys can dream up, in the same way as I need as much obscure theology to inform my weekly observance of the mass. But I really think that I could do with a lot more cynicism and humour about it all. With the exception of Peter Cook's enlivening, healthy English humour, I see little or no contentious cynicism, teasing humour or enquiry about our work in a way which makes us take ourselves slightly less seriously than we ought and goodness me, this has been a serious afternoon.

ROBERT MAXWELL: Well, Peter Pran have you got something cynical to say?

PETER PRAN: I remember a discussion I had with Peter Eisenman three years ago in which I said that I don't want to be an intellectual freak over in a corner, I want to build, just like Mies and Corbusier. I worked with Mies for three years, and I admire how he could relate to clients. It is very important to communicate with clients, otherwise we are not going to get anything built, and I think it's better to use the word 'modern' than 'Deconstructivist'. I don't know a single client that understands the word 'deconstruct'.

ERIC OWEN MOSS: The clients are the reactionaries.

PETER PRAN: OK, the clients are reactionary, but I think it is important to use the right word. Personally I am a socialist, but if I used this word in America I'd be slaughtered, because people hate it. But if you say I'm for free education, I'm for free health they say 'Oh yeah, I agree with you.' So it's a question of using the word to communicate with clients. I really get furious when architects are afraid of criticising each other. But I think in the course of architecture we must stand up and speak against it. The earlier modern pioneer architects put forward an incredible amount of substantive work, often in a struggle against considerable opposition to design and realise their progressive visions. The best modern architecture of today is in many ways substantially different from the earlier modern architecture, but it could not exist without it. Today our challenge is to be explorers in a further major development and enrichment of today's modern architecture; to pursue new courses that represent our society now and in the future. Theory and experimentation are the most basic, necessary underpinnings without which no work of major importance can be created.

The goal is that the new modern architecture be accepted and supported by clients and the general public. As Mies's and Le Corbusier's influence has spread all over the world, it is crucial that all excellent modern architecture should spread in a similar way, becoming part of the lives of people everywhere.

ROBERT MAXWELL: I think Peter is saying in a very broad way what I felt when I saw that Philip Johnson had just come up with a Deconstructivist work.

CONRAD JAMESON: Having one more battle for nationality does not help the question as to where theories belong in architecture. What we are looking for is a discourse for a conversation about architecture, and historically this discourse was political, with a very small 'p', how we live, what our values are – this is what politics means. Now, if we lose this discourse, you are going to get a substitute, and that substitute is theory, which is a lower order of this discourse. Now we can't even discuss what kind of city we want.

Coop Himmelblau, Open House, Malibu

ROBERT MAXWELL: Could you explain why we are in danger of losing this discourse, particularly today?

CONRAD JAMESON: If I could go back to my very first comment, there has been a tremendous import which I don't think architecture can handle. It is over stimulated with ideas coming in from Deconstruction.

DANIEL LIBESKIND: What we are really saying is that architecture is completely underdeveloped. It is a field that doesn't have enough going into it in order to cope precisely because . . .

CONRAD JAMESON: I think you are saying impractical things, you are getting 'overstimulation' and 'understimulation'.

ROBERT MAXWELL: An 'over' and an 'under'?!

CONRAD JAMESON: Today, the difficulty is that we can't find a discourse to bring into the conversation – what theory means, how you see it, whether we need it at all. If you go back to those questions again and again, then you're not going to have a conversation, the conversation simply stops.

LEBBEUS WOODS: Which is exactly what you are doing. You keep coming back to this.

CONRAD JAMESON: No, a discussion asks about our cities.

BERNARD TSCHUMI: The people in this room whose work we have seen – Hani Rashid, Dagmar Richter, Itsuko Hasegawa – all deal with a certain theoretical approach, all produce architectural work whether it's built or not built, all address the question of cities, and probably would not take the idea of values and the idea of political discourse with a small 'p' in the same sense as you would. Nevertheless, this it is one of the most active periods of production in architecture this century. In every field there is a discussion between 'specialist' architects who are trying to figure out the relevance of certain issues. As Peter Pran said, there is indeed the question of translation for the client – we all have to do that – but it's not the context of thisconference . We are talking about theoretical and experimental issues and not about public relations.

ERIC OWEN MOSS: I understand from listening to you for about an hour why you are sitting with your back against the wall, because that is where you are. And I think what you are asking for is to hear a discussion that you've already heard, because that is the one with which you are comfortable. You know where the discussion will resolve itself, you know where it is going. I am not as pure as you, but I'm prepared to say that if it's open ended, I won't wish it to be closed and I don't want to force the discussion to where I would wish it to be. So your argument is wish fulfilment, and I'm sympathetic to your need for comfort and reassurance; but if there is none then we could just as well say let's get rid of Kafka. What is his discourse?

PIERS GOUGH: I think we have got theory and personal belief very muddled up. What most people's theories in architecture are to do with is an ability to operate, and why we have no Mieses and no Corbs now is that these theories lack generosity. We are all thinking how can we make a theory which can make it possible for us to work. We seem to be generous, we go around the world giving lectures telling everybody about our theories. God forbid anyone might copy them or be influenced by them because that would undermine our work. I've never seen so many self-seeking, self-centred, self-interested people in my entire life as the architectural fraternity at the moment. I'm part of it, for God's sake, but that is our situation. For the white-shirted ex-student working down the road in a real office trying to design an out-of-town shopping mall in Atlanta, all this theory and experimentation bears very little relationship to what he finds himself confronted with. I think that what's happened is that the thinkers of architecture have dissociated themselves from the practice of architecture as much as possible, so that they cannot be damned with it. No one could claim that any of us round here could possibly have any responsibility for Canary Wharf, because we've never dealt with the issues about large high-rise buildings and cities. Look at the RIBA, look at us all. We give all our prizes to single-storey sheds because they are elegant and beautiful. If anyone tries to do a five-storey building, it's ugly, it's gross, it's impossible. We don't confront the big issues, we confront the little issues. Our ambition is to work and our ambition is fundamentally that almost no one else should be able to do it like us. What's so joyful about Corb is that he had some generosity of spirit in his theorising; it not only informed his work but was simple enough for other people to use it too. I don't think we have any of those qualities in theorising today.

DAGMAR RICHTER: I think you have proved exactly the opposite of your point by saying that the student in the white shirt is confronted with a specific task. I think that is probably exactly what theory has accomplished, and it is an interesting and positive accomplishment: that student is not blindly sitting there without criticism or any intellectual framework to define what is going to be done with that shopping mall in Atlanta; the understanding that there is a confrontation going on is exactly what theory has produced.

DIMITRI FATOUROS: There seems to be a total confusion; there isn't such a thing as a theory about everything. Theories are very complicated, very multidimensional; they are ambiguous systems, but we are speaking of just one theory. Let us try to define this confusion a bit. Somebody just said that 'architecture has specific theory'. What is this 'proper domain' of architecture? Do we really have a specific domain which is not only construction and which is not only concepts? Neither construction nor philosophy is architec-

L to R: Dinner in the Friends Room at the Royal Academy of Arts

tural; nothing is alone architectural, so let's speak about a very complicated system, a body of things related in theory. There is so such thing with a big theta in Greek – a capital 'TH' in Latin languages – so there is no one theory. Everybody is speaking of just one thing. OK, we have a problem with high-rise buildings, and of course there is a huge problem with the continuous accumulation in the business core of gigantic buildings. This is the 'tissue' of a city, and it is a very critical part of architecture, but another part is how these concepts are transformed into physical space. So I think that we are dealing with confusing situations and if we need to communicate with clients, this also calls for different medicine. We must have a theory for the client and a theory for the masses; we also need a theory with which we may communicate between one another; we are not communicating with one another now: each one is using his own terms.

ROBERT MAXWELL: Well we are not communicating as well as we should be this afternoon, but on the other hand we are not completely not communicating either, and that is the way it has always been with me. I would like to ask Bahram Shirdel to make a brief presentation. You may have noticed how much the temperature has gone up since we started; this is due to the heat of discourse and I apologise for it.

BAHRAM SHIRDEL: I have to confess that I am not in this business because of either theory or experimentation. I am a practitioner and I also understand that in the office one has to experiment, or perhaps younger people than myself in the office want to experiment, and we also have to deal with theory.

I have been basically working with a certain understanding that there are very specific and defined theories of space in architecture. Traditional urban concepts and architectural typologies are grounded in a desire to produce an ideal city as a permanent goal of perfection. In classical European cities characterised by slow regional economies and domestic technologies, such models were perhaps appropriate. Today, however, because ideal city models are static, inflexible and conceived in terms which are no longer applicable to contemporary cities, they are counterproductive to the very flux upon which the city depends and from which it gains its political identity.

Typically, urban planning has understood the city primarily as a two-dimensional phenomenon, concentrating on ground level as the fundamental datum. The three dimensional character of the city is considered only in terms of the impact at street level. The result is an urban planning confined to setting extrusion limits for vertical elements and, in some cases, establishing design standards governing style and ornamentation of buildings. The result has been that developing cities today are virtually indistinguishable.

For the design competition for the Montreal Central Business Centre, we proposed a generalised urban field consisting of three components: the existing landscape, the urbanscape, and the urban form. In this conception, the landscape is not a passive pedestal upon which the city rests, but an active aspect of the full three-dimensional urban field. It is conceived as a network of public indoor/outdoor urban spaces which functions to engender an event structure zone. As a dynamic asymptote, the urban form would provide a three-dimensional form towards which the city would tend, shaping and conditioning new development in a directed but non-totalising manner. All new building would participate in the production of the urban form, while at the same time retaining the freedom to explore individual character.

Another particular project was a competition in Nara, Japan, which a number of architects who are actually now sitting in this room, like Hans Hollein, Thom Mayne and Eric Moss, also participated in. Although it started with the interest in the promise of the commission, we were also dealing with the very

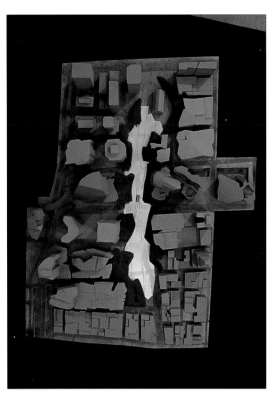

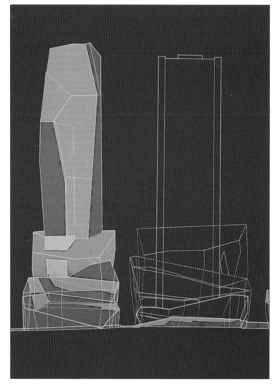

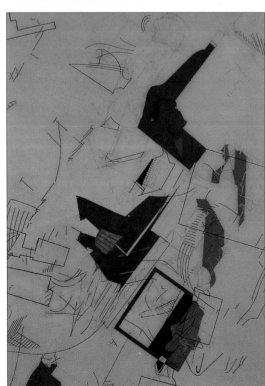

*Bahram Shirdel, above: Montreal
Central Business, Canada; below:
Metapolis, Los Angeles, California*

specific mathematical theory of René Thom. This showed us new possibilities in terms of defining a specific idea of space, which this mathematics also describes as 'fault' or rather 'catastrophe' theory. This is a word difficult to use in dealing with architects, maybe even more difficult than 'Deconstruction'. Our interest is in the possibility that this theory describes of being able to explain unpredictable change in the course of events, and we were interested in manifesting that unpredictability in terms of the space of the building, in terms of the different events that the programme was dealing with.

ROBERT MAXWELL: There must be someone here full of indignation who would like to get some of it out?

ELSPETH HAMILTON: I'd just like to get back to the first remarks that were made this afternoon, which were the opening words of *Metaphysics*. I think that it was mentioned that 'people don't really want to know', in response to the words 'people want to know', and it seemed that there was a general consensus in the room that you do actually want to know something. I think that is missing the point about Metaphysics. Of course that space was filled with objects, and an epoch has spent its time trying to understand the object that it placed in the space of understanding. I'd like to turn to another person, Heisenberg. Heisenberg gave a warning to everybody that we know a fantastic amount already but we understand very little. And he was actually asking for a third speaker's comment on geometry, I believe, which was that to understand geometry is to understand the energy of creation, to understand how one defines or measures an initial creative force. Those are just a few comments I'd like to make about the contributions that have been made.

ROBERT MAXWELL: Thank you. Knowing and understanding. Daniel, would you like to comment on that?

DANIEL LIBESKIND: Well I think it is a very old dialectic between knowing and understanding; it is a very Germanic, Hegelian sort of vocabulary which I don't quite understand because I think what has happened is that the desire to know has gone out of alignment with the desire to understand. So we really get back to architecture in a more fundamental way because the word architecture itself has the word 'arche' in it, and arche is the ultimate underlying logos for something which we now find missing in our own practice. The fact that the world is becoming a world without a principle is something worth thinking about, and that lament for missing Corbusier and the missing greatness of architectural theory, the mastery and domination of the city. I think quite on the contrary we are now in some way out of control, and therefore we are part of the world again. Architecture I think is rejoining everyday life in the sense that it is no longer able to find the principle of life; I would even go further than Robert Maxwell, citing the existential limits of death. I think even this existential philosophy is about the past because we are entering an inexistential philosophy, a philosophy where existence itself doesn't play the same role: it's not based on an individual coming into being. So I think we are really in a very much more radical underlying conversation and we should pay a little bit of attention to the things that are not going to get easier but are going to get more difficult. They are not going to get more clear, they are going to get more confusing, and why shouldn't it be so? I believe in an apocalyptic and radically optimistic view of what will really be happening as we really enter the 21st century. Free of the metaphysical luggage, the demons, the horned phenomena, the magic, the oppressive and repressive professionalisation and specialisation. Architecture will be everyone's, it will no longer belong to someone. Isn't it true that we are finally limited by the ultimate biblical taboo on the Babelian space? Of course, it was just when nations of all kinds gathered together that their effort failed. What is the difference between so-called Japanese space and London space and the space of Berlin? I think it's really the same, even though I don't live in Tokyo and I am not familiar with it. And the space of Berlin is like Tokyo and New York is like Berlin and it is a mammoth Babelian motif which we cannot escape from this time.

ERIC OWEN MOSS: Maybe the question is whether we can add to the confusion or at least try to sort it out. But given the remarks that you just made, which certainly add total confusion, I wouldn't mind it you could explain that comment about existential to inexistential.

DANIEL LIBESKIND: I am very happy to comment on the existential. You were the one who cited Kafka . . . you were the one who cited Beckett.

ERIC OWEN MOSS: I am not withdrawing the statement. I'm asking if you are saying Kafka is a post-existentialist?

DANIEL LIBESKIND: I would say Kafka is the ultimate inexistential . . .

ERIC OWEN MOSS: Have you read his letters to his girlfriend?

DANIEL LIBESKIND: Of course, I know Kafka very well. Let me just what remind you of what Kafka said in those very letters to Felice. He said we have worked for a very long time – he meant for thousands of years – on the positive; now is the time to look at the other side. And that was not a nihilistic comment by any means and just because we are adding to confusion in your sense doesn't mean we are doing anything bad. It's actually the most optimistic thing because we have already seen the kind of clarity that is associated with Albert Speer and Totalitarianism in the 20th century.

ERIC OWEN MOSS: I think what I was asking for was just a kind of honesty which has to do with trying to see what you see and put it down. I think Kafka did that, and he raised the issues which Job raised, so Kafka isn't so new; the problem is the same, it's just stated differently and it's answered differently.

DANIEL LIBESKIND: The problem faced has changed.

KEVIN RHOWBOTHAM: I think we're about to face an incredible difficulty because the common currency of our discussion is a notion of space which we assume is something simple and straightforward, but it is about to disintegrate. Because space seems to me anyway to be increasingly a superstition.

ERIC OWEN MOSS: The apocalypse is always coming for every generation.

KEVIN RHOWBOTHAM: But it's not apocalyptic, it's quite the reverse, it's a creative opportunity. What we've got to stop doing is looking at space and looking at the way we translate it as something transparent

ERIC OWEN MOSS: No question about it.

ROBERT MAXWELL: The fact is, we all know, your creative opportunity is my imposition. Everybody who can do it seeks the space to do it, and clearly we've got a guy who can do it very actively. The next thing I want to say is that we should not finish this discussion without calling on one of the most advanced architects of our generation and of the German speaking nations, Wolf Prix. I'm putting the finger on you because in a way Germany has become the intellectual leader of Europe, so we're looking to you for some network.

WOLF PRIX: At the beginning of the conference I was very desperate because we, Himmelblau, have no theory. Now I start to be very proud of that fact. And I want to talk about a situation I'm very scared about: the gap between theory and reality. From my point of view it's a bad situation because it splits the head from the body. I read a book about the new brutality in schools and the concept of this book is that the kids are so abused by circumstances that they can't feel pain because they don't feel their bodies. If we split theory from building, I think the same will happen to architecture. We see more and more virtual reality, and it is not by chance that architecture now – and I can read it in the work of the students – is becoming escape from reality, and I think one of the hopes of theory could be that it bring reality back into built space.

ROBERT MAXWELL: I think that has to bring us to the end of this afternoon. Obviously there are many things left unsaid, and that's good because that gives you something to say later on. We're glad to see that the RA, after some pioneering work done by Hugh Casson some years ago, is now very close to accepting architecture as an on-going art, and you may notice that this year the architectural aspect is no longer penned into a room at the end with directions and notices saying 'danger' but is spread through most of the exhibition, treated more as an equal, and this would seem to give some force to Daniel Libeskind's contention that the actual definition of space on the ground is a form of the discourse – which would allow the word 'discourse' to follow into spaces where it otherwise might not go. So 'thank you' to the Royal Academy.

L to R: Andreas Papadakis, Wolf Prix and Bernard Tschumi

PETER EISENMAN
THE AFFECTS OF SINGULARITY

There are two English words, 'affect' and 'effect', that sound alike but mean quite different things. *Effect* is something produced by an agent or cause. In architecture it is the relationship between some object and its function or meaning; it is an idea that has dominated Western architecture for the last 200 years. Since the French Revolution, architecture, in its political, social and economical sense, has dealt with effect. If it is good it is effective: if it is good it serves more people. The clearest example of effect is the utilitarian creed of modern architecture; form follows function. This argued that a socially viable programme, properly elaborated, would provide good architecture. Affect, on the other hand, has nothing necessarily to do with good. *Affect* is the conscious subjective aspect of an emotion considered apart from bodily changes. Affect in architecture is simply the sensate response to a physical environment.

Effect can be contrasted with the word affect in many different contexts. This is particularly true when it comes to mediated environments. For example, when I lecture in a foreign country, everyone listens with headphones to a technical translation of my words. This experience is different from the here and now of a physical place: the earphones diminish the affect of my live voice; its emotion, animation and spirit. At the same time the translator desperately tries to tell the audience what I mean. And what I mean is precisely what is at issue. The audience feels it must understand what I say – it must have an effective response to my presence. But I want them to feel my presence, my affect. Like the audience at my lecture, people all over the world are also walking around with headphones listening to rock music, losing the affect of being in space. The loss of the individual response to unmediated stimuli is one consequence of the phenomenon.

The same loss of affect appears when we watch television. For example, for sporting events there is something called instant replay which allows you to watch the play over again in slow motion. Now, in the actual arenas there is also instant replay because people are so attuned to watching the slow motion they can no longer see because of the speed of the actual event; they begin to cheer only after they have seen the instant replay. This is because we have all become junkies of simulated reality rather than the reality of the event itself. For example, after the kick off, in a recent Super Bowl of american football, the players all piled up but the referee blew his whistle and said, 'No play'. What was wrong? The television camera was not ready, so they had to go back and kick off again. The question arises: 'Is this real or is it a mediated event?' And the effect of this non-human mediation is very real; it has become another kind of affect in itself.

The same thing happened at a wedding a year ago. As the bride was coming down the aisle (they were filming for home video use), suddenly the producer said, 'Cut, okay, go back. We need this again.' And so the bride stops, walks back and comes down the aisle again. This continued through the whole service: the exchanging of rings, the 'I do's' and the kiss. The question, again, was whether there was ever a real event because it looked rather like a rehearsal for a video tape. Perhaps the only time the real wedding would be seen would be on the edited video tape, in which case the edited video tape would become the reality. In a similar sense, just this year, in a beauty contest being taped for airing later, they had to shoot two different endings with two different contestants making acceptance speeches and pretending to be happy about winning. This was done because the judging had not taken place. Again the affective reality of the event lay in the video tape.

Another agency that contributes to this loss of affect seeping into our homes is the '1984'-like creature called CNN, which is everywhere on the globe bringing 'instant' news. I remember one night at home before dinner two years ago when I was suddenly watching the bombardment of Baghdad. This action was interspersed with soft drink and travel commercials. I remember the grotesque paradox of watching people being annihilated live, as if for television, only to be interrupted by 'normal' life: buy a car, have a beer. Sitting in front of the CNN television news, one is practically anaesthetised to an affect. Does one believe the commercials or the live bombing? Is it possible to know what is real in such a situation and, therefore is it possible to have any affective response to such a juxtaposition? That is not to say that simulation is not a form of reality. It would be ingenuous to say that what

Department of Art, Architecture and Planning, Cincinatti, Ohio

is on television is not real, that it is some form of child's nightmare, a Grimm's fairy tale brought up to date. But if this is the case, that we are uncertain today what reality is, then it is also difficult to understand what architecture is, because architecture has traditionally been seen as the home of reality.

This is addressed by Walter Benjamin in his essay, 'Art in the Age of Mechanical Reproduction'. Benjamin says that a photograph is clearly an original, although a different kind of original from that which, let us say, is crafted by hand. In one sense the art or the craft product such as, a handmade piece of furniture or a handmade book is different from a book that is made on a mechanical press or a piece of bentwood furniture – which is reproduced many times. But in another sense they are both original, the craft product being individual and the bentwood furniture multiple.

Now there is a difference between repetition in mechanical reproduction and repetition in electronic reproduction: this is the difference between a photograph and a telefax.

The photograph is mechanically produced; it is a product of repetition. It is not a unique handmade artifact; that is, it is not an object of art as craft. The mechanical paradigm dealt with the shift in value from the individual hand, as in the hand of a painter as an original maker, to the value of the hand as intermediary, as in the developer of raw film; from the creation of an individual to the meditation of the multiple. The photograph can be manipulated by an individual to have more contrast, more texture, more tone. Thus, there remains within the mechanical repetition of a photograph a unique, individual quality; it remains a particular object even within the idea of the multiple. And within the process, the individual subject is still able to effect as well as affect.

In electronic repetition, that is the telefax, there is less human intervention, a less value-added dimension by the individual. Further, the condition of the original is thrown into question. Whereas one can agree that there is an original negative plate for a photograph and that this plate can be reproduced, there is no negative plate in a telefax. The original that may be on a disk in a computer; it is no longer an object but rather a series of electronic impulses stored in a matrix. Even the disk original is often modified by corrections, and thus a unique individual original is hardly ever kept. And in fact now, with telefax, the original may not even ever be sent so as to not confuse the reception with the reception of the telefax.

The nature of both repetition and originality changes from mechanical reproduction to electronic reproduction. The change in the nature of originality effects a definition of singularity.

Thus, it is difficult to know what reality is, the reality as the former notion of reality, as the scientific, the organic, the anthropocentric notion of reality that existed in the mechanical paradigm. But if it can be said that if only by virtue of the relationship of media to reality that reality is no longer homogeneous but rather heterogeneous, then there are possibilities for conceptualising architecture.

Within the mechanical paradigm the subject's relationship to the object was clearly understood since the mechanical paradigm evolved from the classical anthropocentric, organicist paradigm. There was a continuity; that is, with every change there was a homogeneity within each paradigm. The individual knew how to react to the object, even though the individual became clearly displaced from his or her centric position. It can be argued that architecture, even though it deals with the same physical individual with the same functional needs and the same need for an affective response to a physical space, no longer produces the same affect because of the shift of the human subject's relationship to the paradigm, that is, the shift from the mechanical to the electronic.

From the beginning of the mechanical paradigm, that is from the beginning of the 15th century, architecture was considered strong media. There is no question that architecture was the *sine qua non* of the mechanical paradigm in that it was the embodiment of the material resistance to natural forces. In its sheltering and enclosing function it provided not only a metaphorical image but an actual physical image of statistics; architecture stood against natural forces. Architecture, in order to shelter and enclose, was therefore not only actually but metaphorically a symbol of a mechanical paradigm.

For example, in the late Middle Ages, in the Gothic cathedrals and even in the early Renaissance wall churches the symbolic evocation of a town was in the church, was articulated in the body of the church itself; in the facades, the side chapels, the carvings, etc. The discourse of the mass was the discourse of the structure and organisation and decoration of the Gothic church. Now obviously this all changed in the 15th century, with the change from Theocentrism to Anthropocentrism.

Another important change occurred in the 18th century when new functions and new political institutions began after the French Revolution. With the rise of the social and economic state, there was a new demand for architecture to make apparent these institutions through new forms. New building types, for example the library, the prison, the hospital, the public school and social housing were introduced into architecture. Because of this, architecture of necessity became more effective; there was a primary relationship between the object of architecture and the physical programme, rather than with the mediating or symbolic functions. Because of this, architecture began to lose its condition as strong media. While it housed and provided for the functions of society, it began to symbolise these functions less. The more the effective nature of the mechanism became important the less the affective nature of both the medium and the message; the social and political type replaced the metaphorical or the affective type. As the public recognition of these building types became more important, little distinction was made between the type and the unique instance of the type in the individual building. As architecture became more of a public, collective concern, it naturally began to deal with the question of repetition and standardisation.

Throughout the 19th century, there is a development of architecture for a mass society parallel to the development of the new political state. It is not without interest that the modern political state of the late 18th and the early 19th century corresponded to the rise of social and economic institutions and with the beginning of the change of architecture from strong media to weak media. While strong media as architecture was about affect, strong media today in terms of commercial television and journalism, is basically concerned with effect: how quickly, compactly and distinctly can the message get across?

But crucial to this argument, is the fact that the mediated behaviour of today does not come from any personal or individual form of behaviour; it is collective behaviour. Media not only sets out to destroy the possibility of individual affect in order to be affective itself, but also must substitute effect for affect. Media assumes that an affective message must be an effective one and this influence alone has entirely altered our concept of affect as well as individual behaviour. For example, media cannot tolerate the possibility of mistake, the misgotten message, error and untruth, all of which are part of the possibility of affect.

Architecture not only does not deal with affect but it no longer deals with effect as well as strong media. Then how does architecture stand in the face of media, and specifically with the loss of the affecting aspect of individual expression. A possible way of returning architecture to the realm of affect may not be through the idea of the individual or the expressive, or through any kind of standardisation or repetition of a norm but, in fact, through an idea of singularity.

Architecture – now operating as weak media –

needs to regain the possibility of an affective discourse. The term singularity begins to explore the possibility of a discourse which brings to the electronic paradigm what particularity, individuality, personal expression was to the mechanical paradigm. That is a general context for exploring the possibility of an architecture of affect. It begins to suggest a contemporary notion of how architecture which is seen as singular can operate as weak media in an affective way within the electronic paradigm.

One way to approach the question of affect in architecture is by looking at the difference between singularity and individual expression, and to answer the questions: 'Why is individual expression no longer valid?' and 'Why is singularity not merely a form of expressionism?' The difference is at the heart of the idea of singularity.

Singularity, as the Japanese critic, Kojin Karatani, suggests is the difference between 'I' the individual subject and the 'I' which belongs to the general category of everybody. It is precisely the difference between a 'this I' and all 'I'-s that must be distinguished. The attachment of the 'this' to the 'I' does not mean that 'this I', the 'me' is special. Rather the reverse it is taking the ego, the individual subjectivity, the persona, out of the 'me' which is in this 'I'. This begins to distinguish the idea of singularity from the idea of particularity and individuality. In other words, Karatani is trying to take the idea of the special 'me'. Even though I know that I am like everyone else, I am not anyone else. What is at stake here is the 'this' in 'this I' and not the 'I' as consciousness. It is the qualification of 'I', the naming of the 'this I', that is important in this context. What is the this of 'this I'? This applies equally for Karatani from the subject, to the object thing and to 'this thing'. Karatani says that 'this-ness' of the subject and object, 'this I' or 'this thing' has nothing to do with its formal or physical features and characteristics. The 'this-ness' of a 'this I' or a 'this dog' is singularity, it distinguishes it from particularity. So it is the 'ness' of this – the 'this-ness' – that is the condition of singularity as opposed to the 'I'. Singularity does not mean that a thing is unique. As opposed to particularity and individuality which are seen as unique when seen in relationship to generality. Singularity is an individuality no longer able to belong to the realm of generality. The attempt is to move the question of 'I' and the individual outside of a metaphysical discourse the singularity of a thing is inseparable from the act of calling it by a proper noun. Thus the nomination of this thing also begins to separate singularity from particularity.

THE BERLIN CITY FORUM

JACQUES DERRIDA, KURT FORSTER AND WIM WENDERS

In this symposium we are trying to bring together people from different parts of the world with a wealth of experience and a rich tradition of critical thinking and imagination, so that our guests are really forced to focus on those problems which are emerging. I think most of us have some kind of link with Berlin and are familiar with its problems. In order to penetrate the city and familiarise ourselves with it, specifically with aspects which may tend to get lost in the overall picture,we went on a tour of the city this morning which showed various points of interest which may lead to a few questions here.

Within such a forum, the most encouraging thing may be the creation of a public forum, in which everybody can freely participate, to the extent of their knowledge and their capacity to take hold of the problems in discussion. At the same time, there is a somewhat frustrating dimension to this, in that this parliament usually disbands at the end of the deliberations but it does not actually execute the results of its proceedings.

I believe frustration is natural to this forum and its limitations are symbolic of the frustrations that everybody experiences in urban life, namely that they are always on a building site. The transformations are not only disruptors and measures of the incompleteness, they are also an absolutely necessary state. In fact, they are the guarantee of the life of the city. In that sense, this city is now experiencing such an on-rush of life that normal procedures in tools and defences seem to be inadequate or perhaps even disappointing.

I'd like to ask you, the members of this symposium, to give a brief assessment of things that strick you the most, that come to the fore, that impose themselves on your mind as you go through the city, as you acquaint yourself, with the life and presence of this town. May I ask Akira Asada to try to break the ice?

ASADA: Well, first of all I have to say that I feel quite at a loss what to do now because I'm an alien here in many senses of the word. First of all, I am Japanese. This is only my third visit to Berlin, the first one after the wall fell, and, at the same time, I'm an alien because I have not specialised in urban planning, architecture etc. Therefore, I feel a little awkward to talk about the city of Berlin in front of specialists like you.

FORSTER: In the United States they make television series about aliens because only aliens can explain what's going on around them.

ASADA: Yes, if a city is anything, it is a place where aliens can come and exchange ideas and thoughts with each other. A city is basically a place of exchange and people tend to think of the city as a kind of closed community, but it's false because the city is primarily a place of exchange, and as Marx put it in *Das Kapital*, 'exchange begins where the communities end'. The exchange beginning between communities and the city, is a kind of enlargement of this inter-space – this space in-between communities. This is especially true to Berlin, the city between East and West, the city where the people from all over the world can meet and exchange ideas with each other.

Therefore, this forum, including Jacques Derrida and myself as aliens, can be a kind of micro-model of the city itself, and it is only in that sense that I can hope to contribute to thinking about the city in a somewhat new dimension. Now, going back to my impression of Berlin under the wonderful guidance of Kurt Forster, I was especially struck by the polycentric and multi-layered structure of the city. It is not a city governed by one single centre or two or three centres, it is a particularly polycentric city. Kurt Forster talked about islands or enclaves, each with its proper characteristics. These enclaves or islands are not only isolated from one another, there are inter-spaces between them and we can see a kind of multi-layered overlapping of many dimensions and many characteristics. The basic question it seems to me, is how to develop this structure in a more polyphonic, creative way.

FORSTER: May I ask Jacques Derrida to engage in the same theme?

DERRIDA: As a preliminary remark I would say, how grateful I am for having been invited to such an exemplary experience as the Stadtforum. To my knowledge, it's the first time that such a conference has taken place. As if a city – an old city with an enormous history and enormous memory – was in the process of re-founding itself, re-building itself anew. And as everybody knows, when an event of foundation takes place, there is

The Berlin City Stadtforum provides a regular opportunity for people to discuss planning strategy for Berlin, here we present a selection of extracts from the proceedings

no law, there are no premises; in fact the foundation as such inaugurates something, doesn't simply develop or continue the past. But at the same time, this is not true, Berlin is not to be refounded – it is already founded. So this is the first paradox of this Stadtforum. It acts as if we were at the eve of a new city, but has, to take into account an enormous heritage. The fact that you invite – I am talking of you, the German citizens – aliens and somehow incompetent aliens to participate in this reflection, means a lot in general, and to me. Today, founding a building or re-founding something like a city implies a responsibility which has itself to be redefined. What is responsibility? In what way are we responsible? In front of a city or for a city, in front of whom are we responsible? Who is responsible for what? I would claim that especially in the case of Berlin, the responsibility has to be shared by an indeterminate number of people, politicians, experts, citizens of Germany, but also perhaps by non-citizens.

To put it briefly, what is the identity of Berlin? I was struck by the polycentric, the multiplicity, the multi-layered structure of Berlin; nevertheless, this multiplicity has a limit. There is something enigmatic called Berlin that has reference and at least a possible identity, a past identity which was enigmatic because it was already divided, already polycentric. We feel we are responsible for Berlin now, not only in the way we are today responsible for a number of capitals, rich historical capitals such as Paris, Vienna, Prague, Moscow, but because of what happened in Berlin in recent times. For what are we responsible? That is the question I am asking, myself and in general. This morning during the tour I was struck also by the discontinuity, the heterogeneity and by the dilemma of what to do with these scars on the skin of the city. To conceal something in memory would be significant not only for Germany but for the Western world first and for the world in general as a whole. So, I am going to jump directly to what is the problem of decision-making in such a situation.

You insisted a moment ago on the time pressure and there is no decision without time pressure, however long the time is. The decision is always precipitated by the concrete problems dealt with by the experts of space, housing, transportation etc, and the so-called fundamental topics, philosophical and political. Generally speaking, of course there is a gap, and I would like to insist on this gap. Of course, I am on the side of the non-expert; yet in such a situation, when you have to make responsible decisions you must of course be an expert, or at least you consult the experts. Non-scientific, non-expert decisions would be irresponsible, that's obvious. Yet, no expert can make a decision, and take historical, political and ethical responsibility. The decision cannot be made by an expert, but by someone who is not in the situation. So as far as our responsibility towards the city of Berlin is concerned – the name of Berlin, of past Berlin or future Berlin – this responsibility has to be taken by an inner body of non experts. So who are they in that case? The immediate answer is the citizens of Berlin, the constituency, the representatives of the city – but not only them. Of course they have to be part of it and I think that the fact that this Stadtforum is open to the public, is a good sign. But I think that for historical reasons, non-citizens of Berlin and Germany may have something to say and to share in the decision-making, not simply in the technical political term, but in the advice they can give to these decision-makers.

I think the fact that we are here in a strange theatre, with the shadow here on one hand and light on the other, is symbolic. Between the light, the supposed light, enlightenment of the experts, and the non-knowledge of the situation in which decisions are made, there must be a gap. And this abyss is not reducible, it is structural, even if it's the expert as such who makes the decision: between his expertise and the decision-making there must be an irreducible and infinite gap and I think that discontinuity is very significant in the current situation of the Stadtforum of Berlin. I think that when the Stadtforum got under way, the decision of giving Berlin the status of the capital of Germany was not made. It has been made now and this decision will have enormous consequences on the topics we are dealing with here. There is no problem about that, but I would have liked Berlin to have been spared this fate as the city would have been freer to witness everything. Now, with the political centrality of the city, all these witnessings will be more difficult.

FORSTER: You've hit on a whole range of themes, many of which will certainly occupy us. I would like to take up one of the things that Jacques Derrida mentioned when talking about the re-foundation of the city. Cities have various stages in their existence, they assume critical new functions: like the function of a capital city or the seat of a particularly significant institution. Therefore, they re-configure themselves in order to play that new role. There have been stages in history in various places where a gradual enlargement of similar functions has occurred, as opposed to other conditions when a re-foundation was felt to be necessary – a kind of hypothetical new start – and of course there could hardly be a condition imaginable which would have a more compelling reason for a hypothetical fresh start than the city of Berlin itself. Its entire historic condition cried out for this. So re-foundation – what does a re-foundation mean? What would be the acts by which the city is refounded? What would be the decisions and the ideas that underlie such a re-foundation?

DERRIDA: I really do not know. The only law of this re-foundation, if it is the re-foundation of an already existing city bearing the name of Berlin, is the law of Berlin. Berlin is the law. Something named Berlin is the law and we are before the law in that case. This means that being responsible doesn't mean being responsible to something present. We are responsible for 'past' Berlin and the many layers, proper names, works, this memory entails. We are responsible to all of them – all of those ghosts – neither living nor simply dead. We also have a responsibility to the future inhabitants of Berlin. So there is no other law. If there is a law it has to be called Berlin, if it has some singularity, some originality.

I think that today what has been called the city age is finished. We enter, as someone said, a post-city age and of course, a capital today is not simply a solid structure in terms of walls, buildings etc; it is a certain mode of concentration of capitalism, of money, of means, of information, of decision-making. All this doesn't occur only in a geographical site, but everywhere. Some concentration occurs and our responsibility is to be vigilant about any re-constitution of monocentric capital. This doesn't mean that we can or should destroy any capital or capitalistic fear, because it's through some concentration in terms of information, money, teaching, culture, that for instance, democracy can be kept alive. I think that the double-bind – including the element of indecision – the double obligation for Berlin would be to keep the memory, unity, some centrality and the tradition of the city. This is of course a self-contradiction: but I think that self-contradictions have to be accepted here; a decision which doesn't go through some indecision, isn't a decision. A decision which simply follows a number of premises, is not a decision. We can juxtapose the traditional solid concrete buildings and memories and archives without transforming Berlin into a museum.

FORSTER: It may be very useful in a sense, to return to the question of the re-foundation because there is a very important historic precedent. There are innumerable instances that I could specifically identify and discuss as to what measures were taken, and what effect resulted from the deliberate incision in the body of an existing city. For instance, the transformations – almost all of them wiped out by now – in the centre of Berlin made between 1815 and 1840. This amounts to nothing less than a re-foundation and redefinition of the entire centre of Berlin. Not even in London could you have a corridor which would end with the Bau Akademie, and would lay out, in a panoramic

fashion, all the major institutions brought into relief by the planning of Schinkel. All this mind you, not accomplished by drawing a masterplan and then taking 25 years to do it, but by only addressing each instance, individually as in our selected case, and only over time, building more than the sum total of what these individual things amount to. So this re-foundation could be very helpful for a discussion of what interventions are imaginable, not so much where would you put it or what would it be, but also the means. The interesting thing there is that you have the most astonishing reversals. Today it is probably the highest privilege to be the lowest building among high-rises. Perversely, because you're sitting on the biggest pot with the smallest ass. There are many instances where in American cities the government buildings and the central institutions are recognisable for being low-rises surrounded by a forest of tall buildings. The fact that the highest is automatically to be identified with the most potent or the most conspicuous etc, may not hold in all circumstances.

DERRIDA: If we don't need tall buildings it's because of the fact that power is not, today, identified with stone and space but with information: technological information processes, telephone connections etc. That's why the identity of the city, and of anything today, cannot be measured with solid stone, but with technical power and technical devices. So the map is not the essential part in the conception of a city and the location of a building is not essential.

I also want to mention the paradoxes of foundation and re-foundation. First, foundation and re-foundation should not be something that's thought of as romantic, but exceptional let's say, happening once and for all. The foundation and the re-foundation of cities happens every day. Why? First because as soon as a foundation is supposed to have taken place, it has to be repeated in the same tradition: the concept of foundation implies the concept of re-foundation. This is at the same time very abstract and formal and very concrete because each time you do something to a city: say you change a street, add a monument or open an avenue, you transform the whole context and, in some way, re-found it. Now, that's why re-foundation is never self-foundation. I will claim that there is no self-foundation. To found oneself you have to be already founded, otherwise, you wouldn't found yourself. To found yourself, you have to be other than yourself and that's why the function is always in the hands of some other: be it from the state, the future, from anywhere. So the general question is, what does belonging to a city mean? What is in the city, what is located in the city, what is visible, what is not visible? Sometimes what is not visible may belong to the city, but it is not necessarily located in the physical sense in the city. To whom does that telephone wire belong? The very concept of belonging to what we call a city is a problem and everything we discuss here presupposes that we should know what can be identified with the name 'building', and with the limits of the city. Of course we know today what the administrative limits are and what the inner limits are – the different limits of the sections, the neighbourhood, for there are some visible limits. But who can seriously define the absolute limits of a city?

ASADA: Coming from Tokyo, my impression of Berlin was of a huge garden city. Even with the highly populated areas in the east, there's hope. But coming back to the general tendency which Jacques Derrida mentioned, given the added benefit of technology; is the city now resolving into a kind of globe covered with an electronic web of telecommunication, or is it resisting this tendency? I think this problem is closely linked to the double-binding task which you mentioned. You talked about the tendency to turn this city into a glorified network, but are there some remnants that have something to do with the historical destiny of this city?

DERRIDA: Well, that's a huge question. In answer I would suggest that if there is a problem with the city, it's to the extent that there is some resistance to the electronic level of the identity of the place. If there were no resistance, you wouldn't need any more planning for any city. The city would be simply a reminder of the past, an archive. It's only because there is a struggle between a desire for the place, for vocation, for visibility, and for belonging. Although belonging is impossible to define, it's a paradoxical structure. Nevertheless, there is an indestructible, irresistible desire for belonging, for a place, for appropriation, for property etc, and this desire is resisting the electronic globalisation which is also another manifestation of the same desire. An electronic dissolution and everything in association with it, telecommunication etc, is also an extension of this same desire with new forms and new mentalities, less and less immediately mastered. Desire is not in and of itself, the way of belonging is not in and of itself; and this leads us back again to this question of foundation. When I said that there was no such thing as self-foundation, it was not only abstractly philosophical. For instance, who will decide about the refoundation of Berlin? Apparently, the administration of Berlin, but we know already that the State will ultimately intervene in everything which will be done in Berlin because in 12 years it will be the capital of Germany. But as you know, even the German State will decide by itself. The German State will decide everything in terms of money,

investment, organisation and it will decide it under the pressure of the European community.

FORSTER: One could recognise the extent to which these divisions would allow one to talk about the formation of this solution of cities. City dwellers, as opposed to country dwellers have long been transcended. Even the person equipped with a car-phone is extending a living room situation or an office situation to the inter-spaces which would have separated the private sphere from the professional sphere. The typical city dweller is an apartment dweller, and to that extent they have no longer all this constant aperture back to an identity between land, real estate and personality. They are always woven into a fabric that is the product of the civilisation which is represented by the city. In other words, the city dweller can retain the city dweller's status and mentality in the absence of the city. You can ship them out to Connecticut, but they will remain New Yorkers and act on the interest of New York in the legislature of Connecticut. The city dweller becomes an ancient independent dweller of the city as a physical location.

DERRIDA: Once more I would like to say something formal and empty in the form of a paradox. I think it's probably urgent and impera-tive that things remain incomplete. Perhaps the most frightening danger when you make plans for a city, is to saturate space, physical space. With a city which is being programmed rigor-ously, the emptiness, the incompleteness is a very difficult task, it's an impossible task, appar-ently. Any desire to complete a lab programme plan, is always the temptation of experts. Of course that's what they have to do, they have to programme and push their programme to the end, to completion. The danger here is precisely too tight. If we remember that a city has to remain non-identical with itself and is open not only to aliens, but as a place for hospitality in the future, the non-identity, the impossibility to draw the limits and the borders for a city is a categorical imperative. So incompleteness is something to be taken seriously. Of course, there is a bad incompleteness and a good incompleteness. We have to be very careful about this, to leave things unaccomplished. There is something about a non-achievement which is of course a catastro-phe too. Do we have a rule to distinguish be-tween the vital necessary incompleteness and the bad one? Do we have a rule? I think that this rule has to be invented – how to invent is at the same time to programme and to un-programme a city, because a city here is only an example of many other entities. We must at the same time vigorously programme and leave some place for play, for things to be open to what is to come. We insisted on the fact that a foundation was never, could never be a self-foundation, there was no rigorous autonomy in a foundation, not even in a decision. The 'other', in every form of otherness, is always involved in foundation, so what is the place for the other in this programming?

FORSTER: On the one hand of course, the sheer magnitude of the task is the greatest temptation to rush towards a total planning; to comprehend and embrace all of the factors and to push them to the limits of their articulation. In other words, the process of implementation is a process of the dismantling and destruction of the plan, not really of simply pushing the plan forward to completion. So there is something at work here, between the excess of planning, perhaps brought out by the magnitude and suddenness of the task, on the one side, and on the other, working against that, the extraordinary process which involves so many countermantling interests and so many qualifying forces, that in the end it corrodes the plan. But the question is, should one still yield a little bit to the plan?

DERRIDA: We have to take responsibility without following a given rule; without simply developing the consequences of given premises. We have to invent a rule – which is an impossible task of course, but the only responsible task.

FORSTER: For rule and invention, Senator Hassemer?

HASSEMER: I would love to share your views on this principle that not everything should be covered by just one plan, and that you don't try to complete everything right now. But I can tell you that it's very difficult to follow this principle. Undoubtedly this accrual of completeness in this city takes place irrespective of the will of planners, politicians and so on. And so the question really is, if you've accepted this principle as being principally true, in the light of the present situation, how do you define it? Where, in which areas, in which cases should we respect this incompleteness? Where should we see to it that matters are not taken too far?

LEPENIES: Well, Mr Hassemer, the question comes up, if you say 'we', who do you mean by 'we'? We have a mixed interest level between the state, the private sector, and east and west and so on and so forth. Take the island for example, why not leave the island the way it is or maybe do something else? You might be going for this option, but how about the other vested interests? Would they agree to this?

HASSEMER: I think we should not take this as a basis for our work in the Stadtforum because then we stop working at all. Wherever we are,

thinking about the future of Berlin, one has to make a first subjective analysis of one's own goals. You must have the assumption that you can implement what you want to implement because in your own analysis you contaminate your own premises by the assumption that there might be many vested interests and so on to dilute your intentions – make your goals unattainable, unachievable. I couldn't work this way. If, in the Stadtforum, they all had the same goal, they wouldn't have to have any kind of a framework to implement anything because then the consensus would suffice, and really get things going. I think I do understand something about these matters, because on one hand you might have your theoretical goals and on the other hand the implementation. What we have to do, is to find out whether it's factually correct, and then we look for the instruments to put it into practice.

I would like to know from the panelists sitting here what your advice would be in terms of the actual substance of the city, because if you don't express this, then you can't make it materialise and put it into practice. Mr Forster said something wonderful and I'll quote him. He meant this in a positive way, that those who sit on this panel here would have to say things now, as if they were the Emperor of China, but the nice thing about this Emperor of China is that we can send them off again once they have said their bit. My question is, Mr Derrida, where are the areas, the spaces, where it might be permitted to sit back and wait, because it would be very fruitful to sit back and wait? Surely this principle of incompleteness would not be helpful because we have to take decisions and make settlements – that's our day-to-day decision-making process.

DERRIDA: I have no specific answer to such a question, but I'll try to define the principle of a possible answer. When you speak of incompleteness, it's not simply the physical occupation of space. There is a problem of housing, of settlement, a demographic problem – how many inhabitants will definitely be living in Berlin? This is a very serious problem, I wouldn't say the contrary, but the structure of incompleteness refers to something which is not simply physical, geometrical or geographical space. We know, that's a point we emphasised before, that today more than ever, the neighbourhood, the proximity, the vicinity is not defined in terms of physical measured space. For instance, we said that my neighbour may be a friend in New York with whom I communicate by phone or by fax rather than the one who lives a few metres from my house. This means that the openness has to do with a dimension of symbolic, linguistic possibilities, and to open the space or to leave the space open means that once you have defined the rules for a physical occupation for housing settlements and demographic problems and so on and so forth, you shouldn't leave the space unoccupied. The very small space may potentially leave an enormous free space, incomplete space. So we have to take responsibility in relation to art, speech, teaching, cultural events, ordinary linguistic exchange also, between neighbours. How will we organise the possibility for people to speak with one another? And when you speak, you do more than occupy simply measured geographical space, which means that the decisions have to do with the structure of the space, not simply the imagined use or completion, of a geographical space. When I take a responsibility I respond to the other and then I of course leave the space open. So, the decisions to be made have to do with these questions of, let's say, thinking, speaking, inventing, what is usually called culture: the political speech too, the television, the media, the differentiation of the media, you have to take a decision as to the number of, let's say, channels, radio or TV channels. They are structuring the space, yet they don't need much physical space. I wanted simply to describe the heterogeneous structure of the space we're referring to when we speak of completeness or incompleteness.

MR COLLINS: Mr Derrida is saying very simply, that it's impossible to have goals that everybody understands and everybody considers or agrees upon because everybody has different ideas about what the city is supposed to be. And he also says that we can't plan everything because many of these things are not capable of being planned, they grow as organisms do, in different ways. What city do the members of this panel like to visit or what city do they like to live in, and where in that city do they like to live? I think everybody has a different idea of what this city is all about, what a city is and what it should be and what it was. Mr Derrida says that the age of capitalist cities is past but I'm not quite sure that he's right, maybe it will be that way in 50-100 years, I don't think it is that way right now, but I think that these questions at least have to be addressed: what kind of city would each person like each city to be?

DERRIDA: I'm speaking in my own name without involving anyone here on the panel. The city I would like to live in is a city I could easily leave. I'm in love with a number of cities including Berlin, but there is no city I would like to live in exclusively. That's why I insisted on the principle of leaving the openness of the city. This is very concrete, I couldn't stand to simply be an inhabitant of a single city and indeed it has never happened that way. I was constantly in exile, from Algiers to Paris, from Paris to suburbs of Paris, to other cities in the world. This leads to a number of consequences, one of them being the necessity for living in a city, yet not simply being planted in a city the way a tree is planted in a garden.

Nevertheless, I'm afraid there has been a very serious misunderstanding about the first thing I said about the rules and the planning. I never said that there was no rule and you couldn't plan anything. I said any decision has to invent its own rules and this intervention is not simply a subjective solipsistic dream. It has to be shared by others, others have to be convinced – these decisions have to be made in common with a number of people. I didn't say no plan was possible, and no rule exists. Simply, if a decision is a decision, it must start something. It must not simply apply to previous programmes, it must invent a programme. A programme is a new set of rules so we must invent new rules and I think this has happened a number of times, each time cities have been built.

FORSTER: Along these same lines, there is for instance, in connection with Berlin and the inventing of rules, the obvious question about whether one can, on the one hand, claim and make much of the polycentric composite nature, with many very diverse elements co-existing in the city, and on the other hand, when it comes to giving to that city a new next stage in its history, in its function particularly as a capital, then revert to that notion of centrality. Why would it be that certain things are still historically and practically associated with centrality, and that they are the spider in the centre of the web, whereas all other people are the dead flies hanging in the web? So this is very much a question that I think poses itself in very practical terms. The centre of Berlin is very, very small, and it is very small for obvious historic reasons. A kind of split-off has already occurred a long time ago and perhaps the biggest moon that has been split off from this planet and the middle is the Reichstag (the parliament in the centre of Berlin). It's right there, in a sense, implying an orbit around the centre. Now, I think a very obvious question is, should there be many more such satellites, should this be a Saturn with rings or should this moon grow to the size of the planet and so forth? I think these are very practical questions.

Let me just tell you that Mr Derrida really commented on the fact that the major thing here isn't just presenting to you a nice attractive familiar solution, which you might find in any city; the questions and issues which are at stake here are different in their nature. So might I call on some other members of the panel here and give the floor to Mr Wenders and Mr Asada to put up some more targets to be shot at.

WENDERS: Well, this idea came to my mind, that you can best see a city when you are not in that city. I grew up in Germany in many cities, for instance Düsseldorf and Munich; I lived in America and Paris, I've been to Tokyo many times and if I close my eyes I think of New York. I also have some kind of a picture of Paris; I think of my lifestyle there, or San Francisco, or Rome. When I am abroad, and I imagine Germany, then I feel nostalgia for Berlin, no other city in Germany but Berlin. This is why I live in Berlin. And if you try to define this nostalgia, this homesickness for Berlin when you are not in Berlin, and then you come to the city then there is a discrepancy between your feelings of homesickness and your feelings when you are in the city; this really defines your city, when you are somewhere else and think of Berlin. I'll try to define why I feel homesick for this city, apart from the people – that is something you can't plan and define – apart from that it's the fact that Berlin is a city which is different from any of the other cities which I've mentioned: it has a lot of open or vacant spaces. If you are in Tokyo or New York everything is crowded, everything is full; unbelievably full. Central Park is the only space in New York. You have some small spaces in Tokyo, but everything's crowded. It's nice that everything is full and you enjoy it, but when I then think of Berlin I'm thinking about the fact that it's fantastic that you have so many open spaces, vacant spaces. And you feel that you don't have one single fire-protection wall or fire-partition wall between buildings, don't even have a term, we don't have a no-man's-land or some sideline waste, derelict like New York or Tokyo and then you realise that this is what you like about Berlin.

From the town planners' point of view it is outrageous to have some empty blank spots, but I would like to take up what Mr Derrida has said. This is perhaps my role in the way I understand it, I want to plead in favour of these empty spaces, the open spaces, fight for them with words because this is all we can do here because it's not up to us to do anything else. Berlin has a lot of these open spots for historical reasons, due to the war and also the events after the war. We now have this incredible state of happiness that we can do some planning, real planning which you can't do in any other city of the world because they have already undertaken their planning for the future. In Berlin we can plan for the future, this is an unbelievably wonderful task. I envy those who can do this planning. This is a small time span and you should really be responsible for people who come much later and have to live with what you have planned. So my plea and my contribution to this discussion is to keep these open spaces, those fire protection walls between separate buildings, this rim of no-man's-land which came about because of the war: leave it

empty, leave it standing where it is.

I remember I was in Brasilia, a unique example of planning. There are just hotels in the district where I happened to live, because it was planned that all hotels were supposed to be in one district. I looked for the city. I didn't find the city. There was one spot under a motorway bridge: it was the only place in this large grid of city planning where you really had a genuine city, where you had communication, where people had a meeting place. And I thought, well, this is what planning should not be, that people shouldn't have to creep under the bridges in order to find a meeting place. In Berlin there are so many places where people can really maintain their style, and I think this is most exciting, to find out which of these places could be left aside when taking decisions. And I think this is also the discussion of the town planners – where should we maybe put in things, increase the density? We shouldn't speak about where to put things, we should discuss where we should keep things empty or open.

HASSEMER: What is the lesson we can learn from Tokyo? I would like to ask you once again, as a non-expert, what things you suggest we put into Berlin, and what advice you can give us relating to Tokyo.

WENDERS: Well, I'll give you a list of all the things you can put in. But maybe we should hear something about Tokyo now.

ASADA: Well, coming from Tokyo and its densely packed space, I do share an admiration for open free space in this city. But first let me go back to what Jacques Derrida said, namely, the danger of imposing a totalistic scheme over the whole city structure. I think he's right in stressing this danger, but let me say something complementary to it because I think there is another danger, of letting the city be absorbed into a homogeneous chaos brought about by the spontaneous movement of capitalism. In other words, the danger of letting the city fall into a kind of mosaic structure, a mere ensemble of small islands or small enclaves, each isolated from the other. While I do admire this heterogeneous polycentric multi-layered structure of the city, on the other hand, I think some principle of communication, some apparatus of putting those enclaves together, is now needed. We have already heard about a kind of centrality and the possibility of rebuilding a centre or centres in the city, but also I think we can think about axiality or axes. This city has a polycentric multi-centric structure, so what seems to be needed here is a kind of bridge between these centres, a kind of axis of axes which somehow interconnects centres. I think this axis can be something physical like a big road or a big railway, but at the same time this axis could be something more symbolic or something imaginary; this axis can be, not only an urban axis but also an inter-urban axis, continental axis, global axis and why not a planetary axis? So what I propose to you is to reconsider the possibility of the axiality within and in between cities. This is a complementary thesis to the thesis of Kurt Forster, of reconsidering the centre and centrality of the city. In this connection I'm only a stranger, an alien of the city, so I'm just asking questions about what might be the possible axis or axes in this greater Berlin which you have now. What could be the possible centre or centres of this city? That seems to me a very fundamental question.

FORSTER: The city is perhaps, in fact, no longer the site where social, political and intellectual powers are put on stage like a permanent stage set. Why is it that most people today in the Western world would probably be likely to feel, as certainly we would in the United States, that the city has become the theatre of social conflicts, it has become the place where everything that doesn't work in social life is most immediately, powerfully, painfully projected in front of you? It doesn't matter whether the building in the background is the headquarters of the Red Cross or IBM or Citibank or a slum for that matter.

ASADA: Let me be a little simplistic and make a somewhat exaggerated comparison between Tokyo and Berlin. Now Tokyo on one level is a very monocentric city, in the centre of it we have an Imperial Palace, but this palace is not like European palaces with imposing facades, it is almost invisible, completely surrounded by forest, moat, etc. So it's a centre, but this centre is empty. This empty centre functions as a kind of black hole which attracts a lot of people, a lot of money, a lot of everything. Therefore, around this empty centre emerges a strange spiral-like movement, sprawl, which goes on indefinitely, which results in an almost homogeneous chaos all the way around this empty centre. Therefore, we have this monocentric structure which gives rise to a kind of homogeneous chaos around it.

This is one picture of Tokyo and of course people who know Tokyo very well, for example Wim Wenders, have a lot to say about it because I have been slightly exaggerating its negative aspect. But in contrast to this picture of Tokyo, in Berlin you have, I don't know how many, but several centres. And also you have distinct, small, enclaves or islands which Kurt Forster showed me, each with its local character, its own history, its own characteristics. Also, there is a kind of overlapping between these small enclaves, each with its own historical time scale. Therefore I talked about the multi-centric,

polycentric, multi-layered structure of this city as something very positive. There are other aspects too, such as the need to interconnect these small islands so that there might emerge some, if not symbolic, some imaginary relation with each other which enables people to perceive a city of Berlin as a kind of whole and in that context I talked about the possible centres and possible axes. Anyway, I think maybe my description of Tokyo and its contrast with Berlin was a little bit over-exaggerated, so maybe I had better ask Wim Wenders to comment on that if possible.

WENDERS: I was trying to figure out my next answer, concerning the criterion of densification and the potential of empty spaces in Berlin. Well, just think of the kind of intensity. There are innumerable gaps all over the city, with walls that do not exist in other cities, so that there are these empty places, unoccupied places in between. In Paris, you would not have that and you wouldn't have that in Tokyo. In part these are not only empty spaces, but barren land, derelict land, even in the inner-city areas, even in the area of the former embassies. And there are hundreds of these places, in and around Berlin. Whether you walk or go by bike or you go by car, you can pass through open areas. And then you come to the next dense polycentre but with this unique quality that constantly surprises, you end up with something that is open, you see sky.

The quality of this city is that you can see the sky. It's in other cities that you really have to raise your head in order to see the sky. And then, inevitably, you either step into puddles or into dog shit; here you don't have to stretch to see the sky. And this quality of a metropolis, is something you really have to fight for, should fight for. And the way we have it here, along the railroad tracks and inner-city railroad tracks that one could mention – they might disappear because of planning, I would think they should be kept. I don't mean open spaces as such, planned open spaces, no, places where nothing happens, where nothing is being done, where you just go past uncultivated places; this is an experience in a city which enables you to look at the fullness that exists in other places. There used to be a place in Berlin where we put up a circus for a film – there were really green paths across it. It doesn't exist any more, but other places exist with the same quality. It is as if for a moment you step out of a city and you really stop and ask; I'm not just on concrete or green-planned spaces with signs and boards. Maybe that is hopelessly romantic but that such wild places should be kept, that is Utopia for me. In 20 years time, a few of those wild places would still exist in the middle of a metropolis, because then it won't become a metropolis. That would be for me a desirable concept, a desirable notion. Alright?

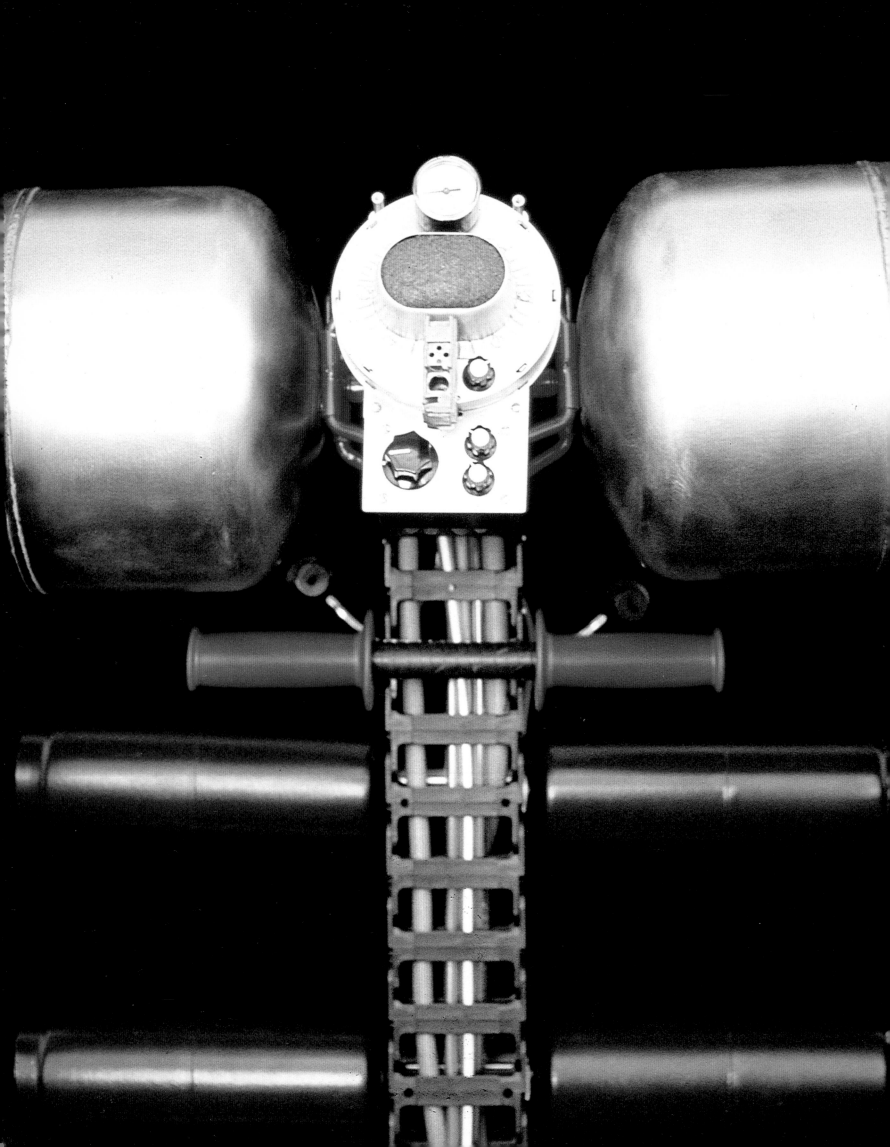

KRUEGER & KAPLAN
ACCEPT NO THEORY, EXCEPT NO THEORY

During the Cold War, we were asked to choose, between two ideologies both antique and neither of our making. Would you prefer the borsch or the beefsteak this evening? Now we make our choices only from the capitalist menu. Architecture currently has a similar menu-driven interface. The fare ranges from the mundane optimised technology loaf to the more exotic, deconstructionist french-fry basket. Given what's on the menus, it seems that we need fewer gourmets and more Cooks. Architecture and politics are both grounded in the pragmatics of Action. But, ideologies in both fields are typically generated out of specific conditions at a point in time. Thereafter, reality is constantly measured against the dogma. Under conditions of rapid change driven by technological development, the dogma inevitably acts as an impediment to a reasonable fit between thought and conditions. Hypotheses are not short-term ideologies. The difference between hypothetically and ideologically-based systems of thought is not only the element of time, but they differ fundamentally in the will to verify and then to modify in an on-going dialogue with the experimental conditions. Theories generated without limit-of-time and without the requirement for verification, become immediately corrupted in application. It is unreasonable to expect that the validity of a theory can remain intact if the initial conditions change. The dissolution of Communism illustrates this hypothesis well. A number of the projects were undertaken in an effort to find an alternative to manifesto-based strategies in design and politics. Projects from the series the 'Renegade Cities' developed under the premise that small-scale, physically isolated yet technologically advanced settlements can develop outside the bounds of the ideologically driven nation-states, in this case in the international waters of the Gulf of Alaska. Further, that these cities act as laboratories of political systems, undertaking investigations far beyond the capabilities of inertia-laden super-powers.

As a development of this research, we speculated about a special breed of city, inspired by the most awesome feature of the Alaskan landscape, the 'Mosquito'. In summer, a two week period in late July, Alaska becomes an occupied territory. Of interest is their ability to instil panic from a series of relatively harmless skirmishes. A nip on the thigh from one of these little units is so invigorating that it has generated the working hypothesis of our archi-political laboratory – the Mosquito. Micro, ultra-lite, and ruthlessly efficient, their ability to infest, inject, and infect is legendary. Their ultimate effect we leave for the political epidemiologists of the future. These cities specialise in short-term, small-scale political structures capable of rapidly acting out hypotheses. Essentially, 'Mosquitos'

reject steady-state politics for principles that are inherently transient, but which provide certain short-term benefits. Conflicts are not resolved but become the irritant that catalyses the next mutation. Within three generations, Mosquitos adapt to any pesticide.

In essence, the Mosquito strategy advocated for political development is an adaptation of the working method used in our architectural laboratory. Architecture and politics are not similar to laboratory physics. Variables are innumerable and are not held constant, experimental conditions cannot be duplicated. As the nature of the experiment is different, new instruments, are required.

As the development of the 'Renegade Cities' precluded our 'designing' them (in the traditional sense), we developed the concept of the analog to communicate about them. Analogs are the architectural equivalent of instrumentation – an oscilloscope applied to the pulse of the specimen. Analogs subvert appearances. They are not models, nor are they intended to convey abstractions. Rather they provoke an understanding of the connections between materials and political and psychological states. The collapse of Communism has effectively quenched the fires of ideological debate on the international scene. This tacit acceptance of a single system based on free-trade and competition now has no real competition, and this does little to encourage a free trade of ideas. One choice is no choice. Communications hardware and software are increasingly controlled by multi-national conglomerates. Many, in addition, are investing in basic scientific and technological research, information bases, recording and film production facilities, and as 'philanthropic' activity, support institutions of higher learning, exhibitions, musical and theatrical events, architectural commissions, and so on. This concentrates the production, distribution, and content of both scientific and cultural activity under the control of a limited number of players. If individuals are to survive this full-frontal attack, new methods must be instituted, new hypotheses rapidly tested and modified, new instruments and tools developed.

Every political and economic system suppresses ideas in order to ensure its own survival. Mosquitos are the by-products of all ideologies. The Mosquitos will find their own way. Experimental political systems are those that embrace short-term provisional hypotheses, incomplete information, and the inevitability of uncertainty. High rates of change are facilitated by the reduced investment in ideological infrastructure.

The essence of the Mosquitos is resistance and survival. Experimental politics, experimental architecture is not an ideology but a methodology.

Opposite & overleaf left: Gasman; Overleaf right: BureauDicto

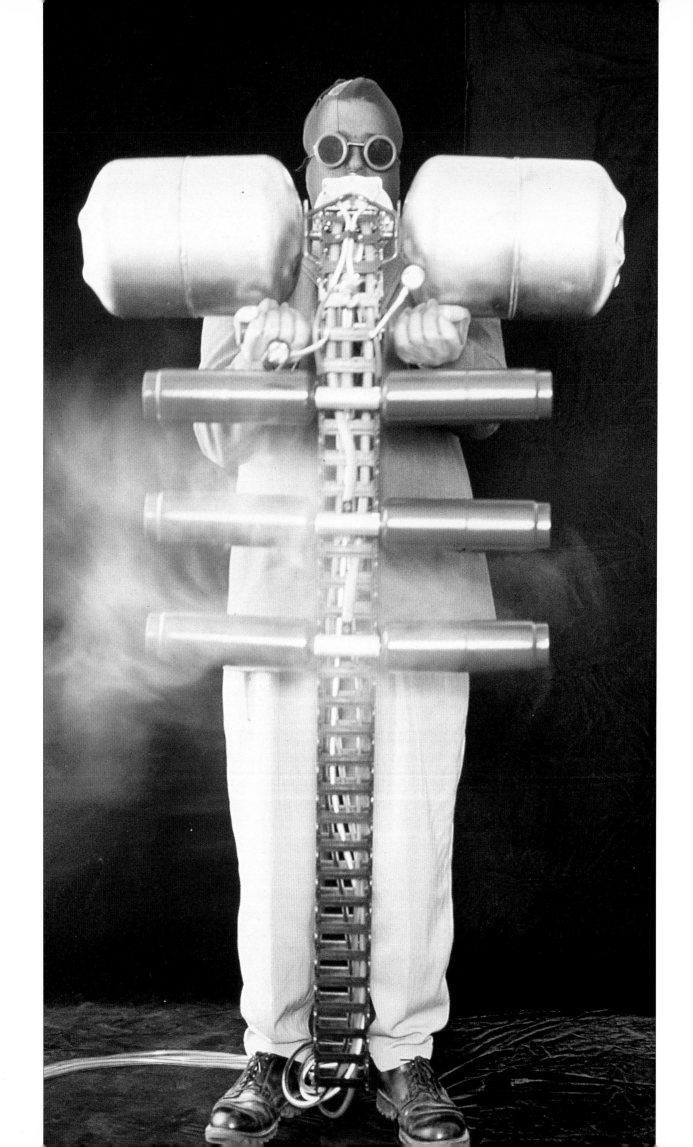

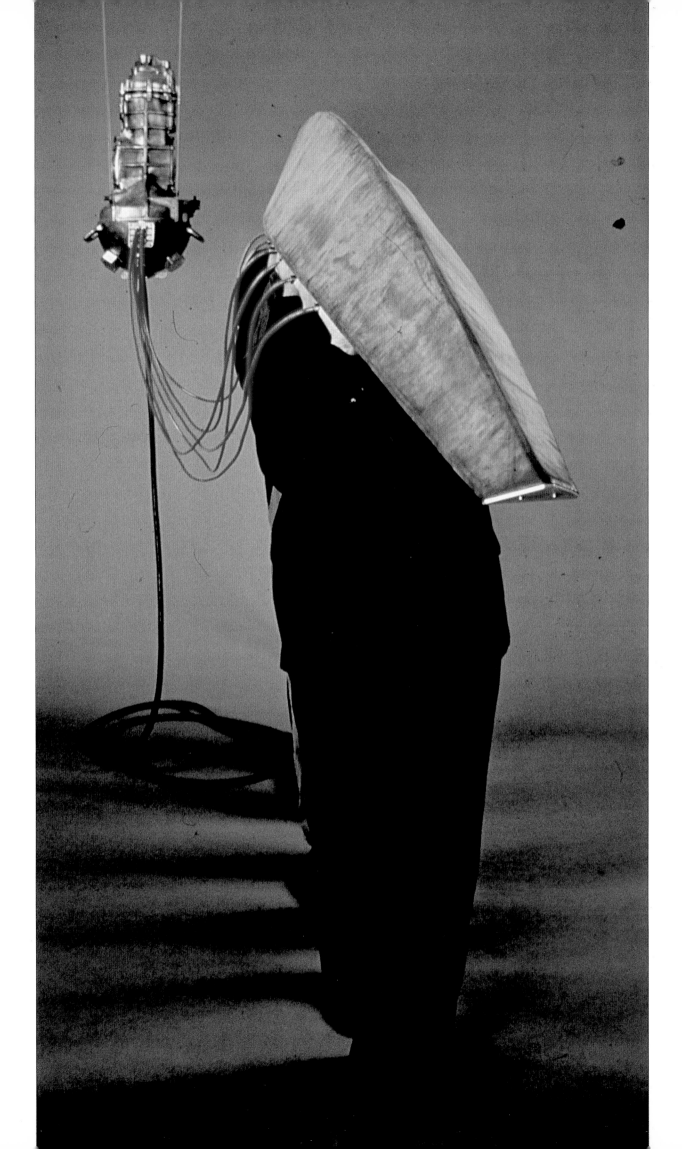

ELENI GIGANTES
VENICE BIENNALE GREEK PAVILION

Set into the banal *tabula rasa* of the Biennale gardens (an undifferentiated, unexploited expanse of grass and trees), this counter-pavilion provides an oasis for exhausted *art lovers* and professional critics during the time of the Biennale, and since it is always open, a landscape diversion for the people of Venice in the 102 weeks in between. Its sole purpose is to provide refreshment, relaxation and amusement, especially following the rigours of touring the various other exhibits. Here it is possible to *incidentally* view a painting . . . or ignore it, in a setting where the simple pleasures and absurdities of architecture can divert us effortlessly when the exhibits fail to do so. Thus *all* the prerogatives of the pre-modern art patron are artificially restored to us.

Laser, video, holographic, cinematic and other projection techniques and the corresponding shift in *avant-garde* expression to exploit these new effects brings into question the wisdom or necessity of replacing a 19th-century institution type (Museum/Gallery) with more of the same: especially in the recurring temporariness of the Biennale where provision need not be made for administration, storage etc. Since the shared physical reality (and historic cross-pollination) of Italy and Greece creates a resonance similar to that of Proust's *Madeleine*, this counter-pavilion seeks to affirm this by giving physical expression to that joyful hedonism that is the ever-present possibility of the Mediterranean.

Resting by the coolness of water, listening to it, watching it, is at the centre of the scheme. Instead of a building there is a pool of water, a flowing liquid platform raised ten centimetres above the surrounding marble ground. The water drops in a cascade as it nears the canal.

Preceding the water, a gridded zone of white marble stretches across the whole site, rising vertically as a 15-metre wall (to receive large exhibits) at the canal end. On the other side is the only enclosable space, where six stepping platforms of white gridded marble descend 140 cm and give onto a pebbled beach which cantilevers over the canal. The beach connects to two zones of marble and enjoys the full height of the waterfall.

Preceding everything are the *tic tics*: a composition of vitrines and benches, artificial trees that replace the missing trees at the end of the green promenade leading to the site. (Though exceeding 'our' boundary, the spirit of this gesture is in keeping with the anti-nationalistic spirit of 1992 and the Biennale itself.)

Exhibitions can be held indoors and outdoors, and much of the outdoors can be glazed and used as vitrines. The stepped marble zone is partially roofed; the wall separating it from the water is a white 'milk' glass cinema screen, angled to correct distortions of projection.

Islands and elements from nature dot the water. A five-metre-high floral mountain has a stream and a staircase to the summit to provide vistas (from which this garden can be viewed – perhaps – as an abstract painting *en bas relief*). The original trees are carefully preserved to provide a *memory*, occupying geometric stepping-stone islands connected with glass bridges: a miniature wilderness reserve. A grid of nine water jets can be electronically programmed to pulsate musically with any tune, and change colour. A seating area is also provided as a pit within the water around which motorised lily pads circulate gently in pre-set patterns.

Finally, a canopy to mark the entrance and a ghost tree over the water seating-area are nothing more than fragments from our *petite phrase*.

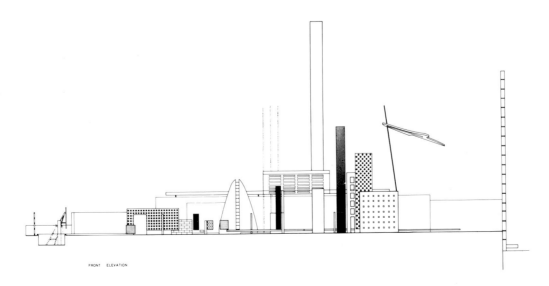

FRONT ELEVATION

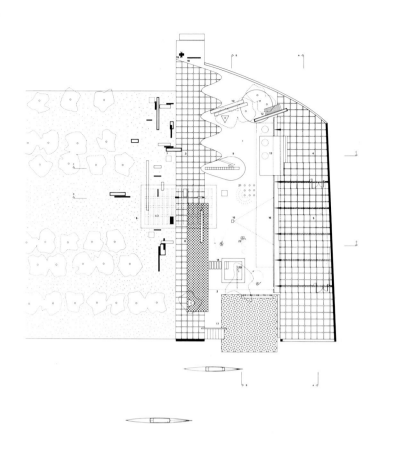

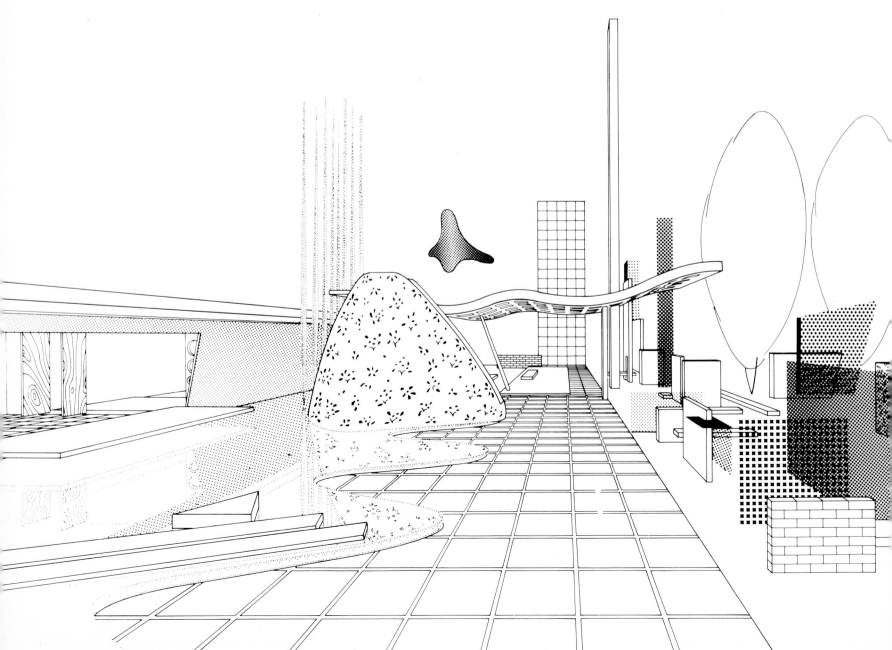

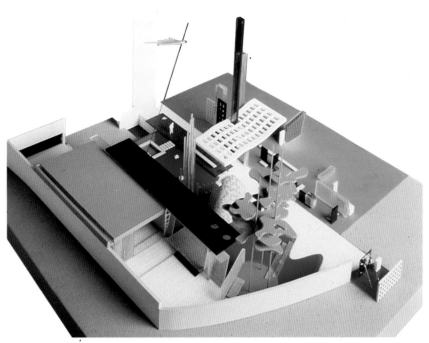

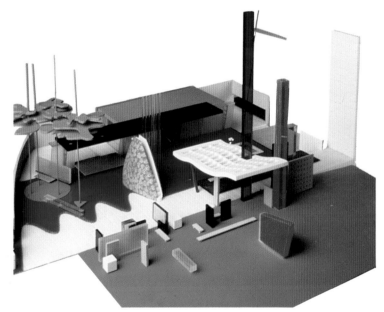

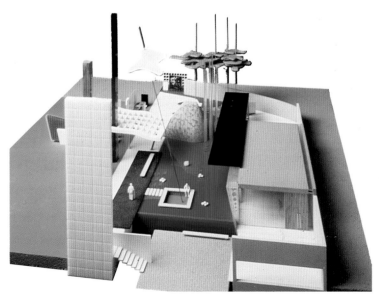

STEPHEN PERRELLA AND TONY WONG
WHETHER CONDITIONS: INSTITUTE FOR ELECTRONIC CLOTHING

The project being developed by studio AEM (Architecture at the end of Metaphysics) is an Institute for Electronic Clothing. The proposed programme's siting is undetermined and aspires to indeterminacy. The non-linear process used to develop the architecture problematises authorship by implementing an invented strategy called *whether conditions*. Meaning here is contingent – nonmetaphysical – and operates as an *other*. The project's meaning does not derive from normative metaphysical relations *vis-à-vis* 'strong' referents, metaphors or narrative structures. Design decisions are *weakly* determined by resonance and effects occurring within specific meaning frames, within and beyond the sphere of the project. Intention does not control the development of form.

Grafting is a technique employed in the whether conditions process to deconstruct existing *texts*. Grafted diagrams used in the initial and later phases, interrogate strong referential meaning. In this practice all aspects of the project are in a *graphemmatic* condition: the condition of two and three-dimensional imagery rendered undecidable. The travelling salesman problem (or TSP, a computer programme based on a sequence of combinatorial optimisation used to approximate efficient travel or marketing trajectories) is one among many of the initial diagrams (glass analysis diagrams were also employed). One discovery revealed that the TSP diagram instigating the inevitable architecture is neither discarded nor strengthened but altered. In the Institute for Electronic Clothing the programme is the *other* of the repressive programmes of contemporary market-driven information culture. In implementing the whether conditions process, diagrams from the travelling salesman problem are graphemmatic devices whose original variables are reconfigured as they contribute to the development of an architectural programme involving electronic clothing.

The travelling salesman problem is scaleless; its meaning configures a variety of references. This affords interrelationships from a global scale to that of microchips: a textual field of information from which to explore the design, location and function of hetero/multi-cultural space. Sites for the project include a representation of the existing fortified walls of Sant' Andrea, south of Venice, Italy, and the Cartesian reference planes encountered in the computer programme SoftImage™ used on a Silicon Graphics Indigo workstation. The process inhabits many sites simultaneously and contributes to the play of the altered TSP programme.

Institute for Electronic Clothing includes documentation of the process and architecture. A *travelling salesman* wearing electronic clothing (a wearable computer prototype currently being developed by NEC of Japan) will distribute fliers offering mail-order digital discs containing a hypertext (electronic) book on the project that includes an interactive request for responses from each purchaser. The material will instigate a limited information network. Afterwards multiple travelling salesmen (with discs) will be placed in tubes and will serve as proposals for prospective clients.

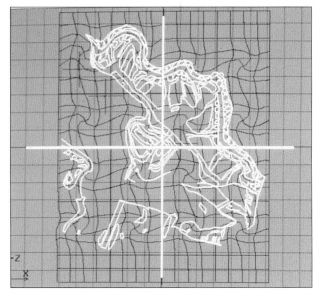
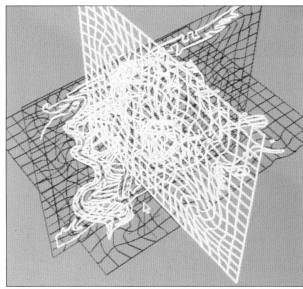

BAHRAM SHIRDEL
METAPOLIS

We were asked by the Mayor's West Coast Gateway Committee to design an urban plan for a large section of downtown Los Angeles comprising of the Civic Centre and portions of adjacent districts. The plan laid the ground-work for the West Coast Gateway Competition. We were also asked to advise the committee on the direction of the competition and the composition of the jury. Our project for the 24 square block area creates a series of new urban spaces which provide the public amenities and physical definition needed to make it a desirable pedestrian area and a civic symbol. Beyond the specific planning issues, our project takes up the question of the geometry and form of cities. In particular it proposes an idea of a city 'Metapolis' engendered by the experience of Los Angeles.

With Los Angeles there exists the potential for a new architecture of the city distinct from any previously realised. It is capable, like no other city, of manifesting an identity which transforms the culture of the world. There is a paradox between the Los Angeles that is built and the LA that is experienced. The built city, understood rationally, relates to the composition of other cities. That which is experienced, and understood intuitively, forms the vital life of the city and is uniquely its own. This other Los Angeles has always existed. It is formed by the aspirations and desires of a people and spirit of a landscape which is wholly outside Western history. It is the idea of LA which persists despite the ideological planning and architectural styles that have determined its physical form.

The Los Angeles project 'Metapolis' is the city trans-formed. It diverges from the history of planning cities which proposes new forms to replace old ones but always operates within the closed framework of form as discreet, apprehensible objects. The plan of Metapolis is realised through an idea of space envisioned beyond form. Space as place (*topos*) is transformed into space in the making (*Chora*). It is the simultaneous occurrence of multitudes of things, separated, without centres, with only beginnings and ends. Each is independent and unrelated to the next in scale, appearance and orientation. *Chora* is a heteroge-neous space created by the occurrences themselves and not a continuum of pre-existing space into which things are inserted. The geometry of the space, the *rune* of the plan, is not a universal geometry. It is a heteronymous, personal geometry which enables us to situate the elements in an open and discontinuous field, the geomet-ric field drawing, which is introduced to the project, supplants the grid of the existing context. That field separates the project from historical strategies of city planning by invalidating the grid as an urban form.

Each independent element of this project acts as a window to the domain of public life in the Metapolis. The public spaces serve as conditions to expand the finite. This project seeks to reflect the identity of a heteronymous culture to achieve the revival of the public in space.

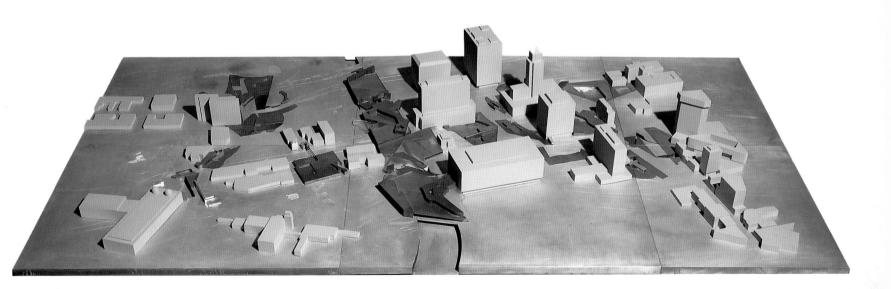

BEN VAN BERKEL
OFFICE BUILDINGS, AMERSFOORT, HOLLAND

The two eyes of the building are seminal to its structure. The 25-metre-long green glass eye in the front facade was the first point of departure; this window had to deliver light to the upper floor of offices. Because the partition walls between the offices do not quite reach the facade, and because this window is kept free also, the effect indoors is of a balcony-like zone. Moreover, the window had to be oriented to the intersection in the industrial zone in which the building stands. This intersection is the only urban factor in the vicinity that lends definition to the otherwise unallocated area.

The small, fully agglutinated eye protruding from the west facade is a physical consequence of the need to deliver more light inside – more specifically, to the end of the corridor joining the offices on the upper floor. Outside, the eye accentuates the rotation of the building. It is at this point that various separations are evident; the upper floor shifts from the ground floor set at right angles to the

building line, while the internal separation between office levels at the front and double-height storage workshop at the back is found here too. Rotation of the second level has been variously expressed in the facades. At the east facade, for instance, there was the possibility of placing the entrance at the point where the shift occurs between ground and upper floor. The interior rotates with the shape of the building. On the second level the shift gives rise to a tapering corridor off which there are offices, and which culminates in the small eye.

The objective character of the building, which stems from the unallocated nature of its surroundings, is accentuated by the way in which the solid-looking ground-floor level forms a plinth, as it were, for the more airy and vivacious upper floor. On this issue the construction methods of the two layers are in agreement; concrete below and steel above. The thematics of space are continued in the details of the interior.

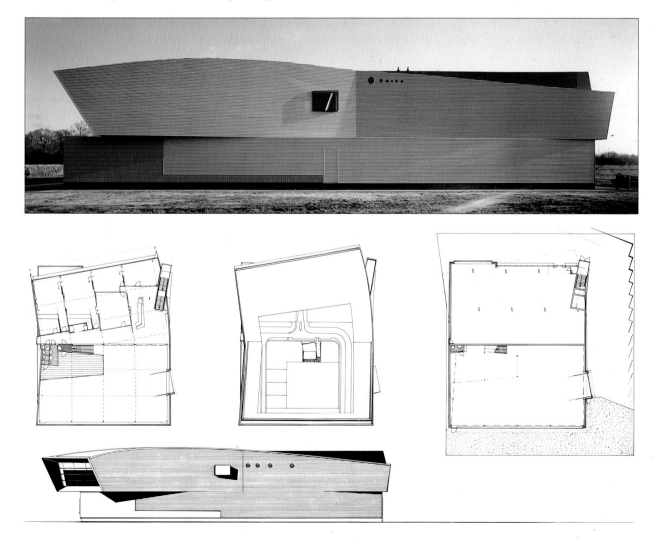

BOTOND BOGNAR

ANYWHERE IN JAPAN

An International Symposium on Space, Site, Place and Architecture

It is not an exaggeration to say that today, at the end of the 20th century, we are living at a particular historic moment when a growing number of pressing issues are profoundly affecting every segment of contemporary life, human consciousness and conduct. To convince the sceptics – of whom there are many – the most obvious example which must be mentioned at the outset, is the alarming state of our endangered planet Earth. We seem to have reached a breaking point beyond which the ecosystem of Earth, the home of mankind itself, cannot withstand any further exploitation of its resources without seriously undermining the very existence of human societies. If this sounds apocalyptic, the Earth Summit in Rio de Janeiro, 1992, has proven that the ecosystem and our natural resources are indeed in a state of almost irreversible damage from which they can only be redeemed through a *global* effort. The harm we inflict on Earth: pollution, untreated waste, deforestation, over population, etc, knows no national boundaries or political systems and ultimately effects us all. Anything anybody does in this regard today has consequences somewhere else. If this is not recognised by every society and everyone (not just anyone) equally, any effort to correct the course of our fate is necessarily jeopardised. Yet we also know that such efforts to improve on the present human condition are ultimately paradoxical. To survive, many poor nations are prompted to benefit from the deforestation of their lands, that in the long run surely undermines the viability of not only their land but ultimately anyone else's; the rich eventually have to bail out the poor.

However, this paradox of the environment is not the only one we face today on our way towards a 'new world' of tomorrow. The new political landscape is equally contradictory. In the past few years we have witnessed the end of the Cold War and the beginning of a liberalisation process that is as promising as it is risky, and even tragic, as the events in the ex-Yugoslavia, ex-Soviet Union and elsewhere (practically 'anywhere' including South Africa, Cambodia or the US [see LA Riots etc]) prove only too well. The redrawing or erasing of the previous political maps (the 'disappearance' of the Enemy) means the shifting of power relations and the potential triumph of capitalism over the entire world, turning it into one global market place on the one

hand, and blurring the boundaries between Ruler and the Ruled on the other hand. All this also means an apparent 'depoliticisation' of the world itself. The question is whether we can live without an Enemy and still be political or if we have to find a new Enemy (Japanese economic progress perhaps).

The disappearance of the boundaries within the political world seems to coincide with a similar breaking down of the boundaries among various disciples and human knowledge even within the fields of science. The tremendous advancement in chemistry, biology, bio-engineering, physics, astrophysics, space exploration, etc, means that they cannot be defined any more within their own, and previously comfortable spheres; they are now merging, almost inextricably. Moreover we see the emergence of new, non-linear system theories, fractal geometrics, chaos theories, and various networkings that evolve by way of the application of new technologies: computers, computer programmes with fuzzy logic, all profoundly challenging our previously 'stable' and unimpeachable logocentric world, human thought and reality.

These phenomena, on the other hand, are not independent of the fast proliferating information and communication systems and media technics that are changing our perceptions about the world. TV and Radio networks, portable telephones and computers, fax machines, jet-fast transportation systems etc provide us with a spread of immediacy to communicate with any part (or anywhere) in the world. These new technologies are capable of duplicating *ad infinitum* just about any human experience or knowledge. More importantly, they are also capable of stimulating experience, so far unknown, thereby creating new *virtual realities* or effectively blurring the boundaries between reality and fiction. As a result, the issue of originality or Origin is problematised as much as the notions of authenticity and legitimacy are questioned.

In short, one can observe a kind of schizophrenic situation wherein the processes of both globalisation and particularisation occur in a dichotomous fashion, opening the way towards multiplicities of *uncertainty* or situations of undecidability. One early example of this is the discovery of the 'uncertainty principle' in quan-

Jeffrey Kipnis

Jacques Derrida

tum mechanics by the German nuclear physicist Werner Heisenberg. These developments in turn appear to pave the road(s) towards the possibility and even the necessity of seriously challenging our world of thinking, knowledge and action, all deeply rooted in, and constituted by metaphysical 'foundations'.

It goes without saying that such changes have a profound and inevitable impact on our culture, architecture and urban environment, as well as on our understanding of them. Consequently the discipline of architecture is being transformed: its definitions expanding while its boundaries with other disciplines are shifting, becoming more ambiguous. For example, architecture has a renewed and intense affiliation with various fields of human thought: social, literary and cultural theories, philosophy to mention but a few. Also, architecture is increasing reliant on the various new, information, media and computer technologies that are now probing the very essence of what has been traditionally referred to as architecture, and more so, urbanism.

It is precisely the recognition of the necessity to rethink the problematics of site, space, place and architecture in general, with regard to the rapid and dramatic changes in our world, that has prompted the initiation of a series of 11 annual cross-cultural and multi-disciplinary conferences by the so-called Anyone Corporation. These conferences are to be held in various places throughout the world. After the first meeting, entitled, 'Anyone' in Los Angeles, California, the second one, now called 'Anywhere' was organised in Yufuin, Japan between June 9th to 11th, 1992. The organisers, Jeffrey Kipnis and Peter Eisenman's office in conjunction with Arata Isozaki and his Atelier in Tokyo, invited a select and small number of prominent thinkers: philosophers, sociologists, psychologists, artists and architects, to discuss the issues facing architecture under the new and rapidly unfolding circumstances briefly outlined above. More precisely the goal was to focus upon 'the undecidable condition of architecture and its relationship to the general culture at the end of the millenium . . .'

Among the participants, in addition to Kipnis, Eisenman and Isozaki, were the French philosopher Jacques Derrida, the Japanese Bin Kimura, Kojin Karatani, Shigehiko Hasumi, the Americans Fredric Jameson, Mark Taylor, the artists Akira Asada, Shusaku Arakawa, Madelin Gins and the architects Tadao Ando, Toyo Ito, Rem Koolhaas, Daniel Libeskind to mention but a few. Some, like Rafael Moneo and Paul Virilio, made their 'appearances' by sending in video recordings of their presentations to be reviewed at the conference, so that in the meantime they could be somewhere else (or anywhere). The setting of the meeting was arranged in the small gallery space of Arata Isozaki's tiny Yufuin Railway Station on

the Island of Kyushu. Yufuin is a remote place in the middle of nowhere (or could it have been again anywhere?). However, as it turned out, it was not just anywhere; it is a small resort town with hot springs set among rolling hills and mountains; nature with an appealing character. The conference was in a railroad station (where else?) with trains frequently passing by. Yet the 'place' of the conference was also somewhere else, both literally and figuratively speaking. Limited as the setting in the small gallery for some 40 people was, the space was linked, connected and so extended to other locations in Yufuin as well as Tokyo, where additional and larger numbers of participants could follow the discussion and communicate though TV transmission (via satellite) and by way of fax machines. In this sense the conference indeed could have been anywhere.

Presentation and discussions centred around the general issues of space, its spirit, its reality, its fiction, and its Anywhere. Breaking down the theme into more specific aspects, the consecutive sessions addressed the topics of 'Definition of Space' 'Site/Non-Site Specific' 'Genius Loci/Feng-Shui' 'Metropolitan Network' and 'Simulated Space'. In the printed announcement the organisers correctly outlined, that 'Traditionally the notions of genius loci (in the Occident) and feng-shui (in the Orient) have served as mediators between architecture and its environment'. And they asked the questions: 'Are these notions [still] relevant today? If not, what is functioning in their place? How can we invent new forms of mediation or even non-mediation for architecture and the city?'

In regard to the increasing phenomena of globalisation and universalisation, perhaps not quite independent of today's proliferation/penetration of information networks, the organisers' statement of problematics continued with both incisive observations and further questions.

Today space is dichotomous: open and closed, outer and inner, public and private, homogeneous and heterogeneous, general and particular, etc. On the one hand, we are coming to live Anywhere, floating on the global network of air transportation and electronic real-time communication; on the other hand, we are confined in Anywhere – in an arbitrary cell of the city as a theatre of memory in ruin. How can we slip out of those dualities and find an new axis connecting hermetic/cryptic – cryptographic/grotesque space and postal/telegraphic-telephonic-televisual space? In other words, how can we conceive the singular-universal axis apart from the particular-general axis (given the importance of 'virtual space')? In that direction, how can an architect cut-up and fold-in (ply/plier) the

Arata Isozaki

Peter Eisenman

71

space? How is the deconstruction of the past hermitage and the urbanisation of the real-time possible?

The main speaker of the conference, Jacques Derrida in his presentation, 'Faxitecture', addressed first of all the most general, yet most pressing questions mankind faces today, asking: What happens to the Earth, what about man and what about architecture? In his statement he outlined that these issues today cannot be appropriately discussed and answered without reference to the new information technology (a position implicitly referred to by the title as well). In calling for a new spatio/temporal structure, he emphasised the temporality of space, the temporary occupation of place, wherein 'place is nothing but the possibility of replacement,' that is to say, place is first of all substituted with *placing* and placing is always replacing. Although this is a paradoxical statement, Derrida also reiterated, that in our new approach to space and place we cannot avoid the application of paradoxical logic. Accordingly he continued, *deconstruction is* an act of *rebuilding,* and as such is an affirmative rather than a negative or nihilistic project.

The following sessions, moderated by thinkers of various 'schools' or convictions such as Mark Taylor, Jeff Kipnis, Akira Asada, Rem Koolhaas, opened the floor for a broad range of views often with heated discussion between opposing parties. Many commentators, calling for the repoliticisation of space, pointed out correctly, that space is always inherently political in nature, yet today this dimension is repressed. It was also pointed out that the notion of 'space' is a historic category and can be associated with the project of the Modern; the concept of space only appearing for the first time in the writings of German art historians and theoreticians in around 1890. It has always been associated with 'architecture's dream of order' and 'dominion over the physical organisation and the order of the social and political field . . .' as 'it predicates life with increasing precision' (Kipnis). Therefore 'Space is not merely a pre-eminent meta-physical notion, but inextricable from the project of metaphysics' (Kipnis).

Although rather divergent approaches were voiced by theoreticians such as Rafael Moneo, Ignasi de Solà-Morales, Tadao Ando, Arakawa, Kipnis, Taylor, Jameson, etc, almost all seemed to agree in their rejection of a rigid and deterministic approach and/or definition in lieu of a more flexible one, interpreting or associating it with action, production or event. In a similar way the traditional interpretation of *genius loci*, where *spirit* was regarded as some permanent and pre-existing or *a priori* quality was challenged by a more *circumstantial* one, wherein the *genius* is also constituted and recreated by architectural interventions allowing room for unpredictable action and events of chance. Isozaki talked about 'MA, Chora, receptacle' alluding to the differing traditions between Oriental Japanese and Western understanding of place, while Ando, in his brief but intensively poetic statement on 'Genius Loci', argued for its interpretation as a life-giving energy and as such, a movement that can transform and renew a place, as he said: 'From place there is a ceaseless outflowing of new life'.

While it was agreed upon that all living beings – and not only humans, as Heidegger implied – need dwelling, the Heideggerian project was also sharply criticised, insofar as many, including Libeskind and Elizabeth Diller, argued against the danger of domesticating every segment of life. Diller was particularly poignant and sharp in criticising the world-wide (and growing) tourist industry which, among other things, domesticates travel: 'Tourism transports the body anywhere without eliminating the notion of home'. Tourism, she continues, is the commodification of both sight and site.

From this notion it is then only a short distance to the other phenomenon of today: the problematics of Architecture in the Simulated City. One of the architects whose work relates closely to the subject, Toyo Ito, pointed out the dangers of new technology. In addition to opening up potentially new horizons for human experience, it also can and does produce mere pseudo-experience. And he asked 'If we are to imagine the future, what other states than the extreme state of technological control can we expect?' This process, despite its appearance to the contrary, is also a process of absolute *homogenisation* of life and society. 'Homogenised contents permit trivial differences in the superficial character' as Ito said. But he also recognised the ultimate paradox of the situation and the dilemma of the architect: 'It is meaningless for us to stand outside these conditions or to take a position where we do not recognise two problems as contradictions . . . We should rather build fictional and ephemeral architecture as a permanent entity.'

Although offering no easy solutions, or solutions at all, the symposium ended with the implicit understanding, that architecture 'anywhere' cannot remain just anywhere, it always has to be somewhere; hence the dilemma that seems to prevail. At any rate, in the meantime, there are plans to organise the third meeting, perhaps '*Any*time' next year, yet not in any other place than Montreal, Canada to which event, as much as to the publication of a 272 page book about *Any*where, we can look forward with genuine interest any time.

Tadao Ando

Mark Taylor

PROSPERO'S SOFTWARE
Brian Hatton

'Wouldst thou be window'd in Great Rome?'
Shakespeare, *Antony and Cleopatra*
'Paris Vancouver Hyères Maintenon
New York et les Antilles
La fenêtre s'ouvre comme une orange
Le beau fruit de la lumière . . .'
Apollinaire, *Les Fenêtres*, (Calligrammes)

Like an orange . . . Or an Apple Macintosh. Apple software has a facility called a 'Graphic User's Interface' which makes its screen show how the computer describes reality. IBM's equivalent software is called 'Windows' and we might say that it opens on a space that is the 'Great Rome' of the communications age: that protean multimedia flux of signs and processing that William Gibson has called 'Cyberspace'. Do the windows look in or out? Like contrasting facets in a cubist image, the answer is both and neither, simultaneously. There is a place of cusps where such oppositions as near and far, large and small, real and imaginary, objective and subjective, public and personal, are brought to wilful interchange that is no less play than process. Nigel Coates calls it 'Ecstacity', a tract with no topography but a mutable semiography, where a lap-top can permeate a district and every limb of the body might link event and space in a '*mise-en-abîme*' of signs and sighs, of streets and sheets.

Like the bed of love in Donne's *Good Morrow*, this architecture 'makes one little room an everywhere', and allows the shopfitter, gardener, nightclubber and hacker their part in the urban masque. Their Disco-verite turns streets of actuality into a city of mightlihood, of wish and vision, a dream of liberation with no masterplan but as many programmes as its occupants' desires. So make no small plans. In fact, make no plans at all. Rather, with angel's eyes in cross-cultural X-Ray, see all plied in one, and one through all, on a skein of permeable situations, a dispersal of operative images across space that might be protocol or precinct; or see both together, becoming new narrative, new devices to be tried, tuned and twisted in the extant city.

We encounter a two-fold task: to discover amid the 'bright satanic market' a new medium of transmundane vision that might bring Blake's 'Albion' to urban life again, and to cast a means of representing it in a room, a screen, a city. Indeed, after McLuhan they are the same, insofar as the medium made vivid is the message made real.

We are to realise the city, as a multiplex agency of media, and to recognise in our infinite and capricious imaging the billowing of a new sublime. It was Piranesi who invented the urban sublime, literally discovering it in the prodigal heap of ruined Rome – a Rome that never was, but might have been and might again be in some stupendous and culminate *Ricorso*, when all tombs, prisons, palaces and pomps would break down into a festal ornament, fertile compost to renewed imagination. But see how the plates of the *Antichità Romana*, with their insets and roll-downs, the plans of the Campo Marzio, with their spreadsheet proliferations, resemble the fantasticating algorithms of some computer bacillus, a programme bewitched.

Today we have no ruins, save those, as Robert Smithson pointed out among the entropic monuments of New Jersey, that rise into reverse – our building sites and incomplete utopias of yesterday's tomorrows; and their element is not earth but air. When Robert Delaunay sublimated cubism into the simultaneous contrast and synchronous movement of coloured light, he called his pictures 'Windows On the City'. Today it is not in lightwaves but in electronically spun languages that the city dissolves and recourses. Likewise, our Rome: no longer retro but imminent, its forum not the cynosure of all roads but an everywhere in the web of all channels; its Piranesi no dark genius but a plural montage.

But an as-yet occluded montage which, with all its show of dynamism, is still lumpen, ill-distributed, subject to mean and narrow powers and yet to grasp the enabling pattern of its own collective prospect. If urban design has any vision, it can be merely to prospect, as in a lode, the gold of desire. In *Paradise Lost*, Milton describes the building of Pandaemonium from infernal metals. In the 1940s, Humphrey Jennings, surrealist and maker of wartime documentary films like *Listen to Britain* which had pictured the pulse of the nation, began a collage of material for a new kind of epic in '*Pandaemonium*'. Inspired by Milton he wrote:

> Pandaemonium is the Palace of all the Devils. Its building began c1660. It will never be finished – it has to be transformed into Jerusalem. The building of Pandaemonium is the real history of Britain for the last 300 years. That history has never been written . . . The present material is a selection. A foretaste of the full story.

From Pandaemonium to Jerusalem, via the Strand and Prospero's Software of consumer culture? Ecstacity, remember, is a 'mightlihood' – it might just be.

JIGSAW (relay: *Body*)
Jigsaw is a clothes shop in Knightsbridge. But let's re-jig the verb 'is' to another tense; let's call it the 'present imaginative', say 'might be'. And let's supplement 'Knightsbridge' and 'shop' with other ideas which we might call 'imagined presences'. Now allow real and virtual images to react with the actual vitality of buying and selling, and let the whole business be seen as a metaphor 'in micro' for a modelling 'in macro' of life lived 'in metro':

73

Metropolis. Now let this entire circuit of representations feed back continuously to itself, let the informing and direction of this feedback become the method of design: narrative architecture, NA.

NA supposes that the morphology of the city could reflect its social neurology. The city is a layered ever-changing figure of processes and elements that, when given shape as architecture, tends to make the city like the body.[1]

Layers, change, process, body: at Jigsaw all are meshed, but let's begin with the body. There's yourself, of course, among the press of others, and as you approach the frontage window you'll see your reflection approaching to meet you, a dim commentary on your own twin ideas of yourself – how you are, and how you might be. There are aluminium mannikins modelling the clothes and the others trying them on. Garments hang on racks that line the side walls like '*culisses*' in a stage set, each one a skin awaiting its potential body. Along the curving quadrant of the rear wall the racks become changing-bays, not so much *culisses* now as theatre boxes, for the quadrant is reflected as a lateral mirror-wall that visually doubles it into an exedra. Upstairs, the conceit is explicit: there's a proscenium at the back, and the changing-cubicles are flanking *culisses* to a trying-on stage. Here, 'actors' emerge to regard themselves, compare with others, and be regarded against a mirror backdrop that reflects the whole depth of the shop and the street outside.

It is a theatre of reciprocal rehearsals. The mannikins too exchange roles: blue glass variants, half torso, half vase, illuminate the stairway, and the theme of body and vessel appears in a ceiling frieze. The body appears as self/other, actual/virtual, literal/metaphor in a chain of presences throughout the store. These trans-imagings are enabled through the facility of the building, which exhibits the same kinds of transmutative double-coding. Return to the frontage, but this time focus on frame rather than figure: three modes of *modus operandi* are at work, corresponding to Space, Image and Matter. First, a permeating and overlapping of fields to create 'twi-zones' where identities loosen and shift. They occur through layered, translucent thresholds, or by labile and fluid surfaces. One invites movement of the mind, the other that of the body. The second is a metamorphosis of imagery. The third is a relaxed promiscuity of materials and metiers: industrial and craft production intermingle freely.

Jigsaw is a proscenium to the street, but it is also an aquarium, a TV screen, a frieze, a temple, a cave, an avial emblem, a ship's prow. All these things have occurred elsewhere in Coates' work, but their co-presence is enabled by an imaginative reading of their co-presence already in the

world/city of today. They spring from an outlook that knows – indeed lives – displacements and the slippages that inspire the 'deconstructive' turn in architecture, but, not content merely to mimic them in abstract form, turns a deconstructive gaze on such pairs as 'abstract-figurative', 'form-content', 'structure-programme'. The method is playful but systematic, an 'industrial *capriccio*', a volatile yet sustained projection, as vivid as a hallucination, as operable as a computer screen, as palpable yet protean as a lover's body. Hence a motto inspired by an urban vision but as germane to mundane minutiae: 'Configuring Mercurius'.[2]

TOKYO FORUM (relay: *Exedra*)

At the start of Nigel Coates' architecture is an experience of reversal in the relations of 'nature' and 'man-made' that seems to have occurred during his stay in Italy in 1978, and which seems in intuitive correspondence with certain ideas in Adorno and Horkheimer's 'Dialectic of Enlightenment'. Here, the process of alienation from nature that shadowed the growth of reason and subjectivity brings man (and the city) to a point where the city itself, a work of reason that has become purely instrumental, now becomes a second nature, with the terrors and fascinations of the first. Unlike many others, however, Coates finds this a cause not for despair but delight, for it makes again a condition in which art may make anew a clearing for communicative vitality.

This clearing, however, is not one of 'authenticity' in the jargon of Heidegger, but one of facility, exchange, and free representation; it is a stage, a world-theatre in the guise of a garden, a garden composed of urban events and artifacts the way that a traditional garden is made of plants. The Italian garden, Coates noted, was neither formal nor picturesque, but theatrically urban, prefiguring the nightclub and arcade game with 'an . . . almost urban feeling of shuttling, like a pinball machine'[3] and Coates introduced an exhibition of Situationism – its derives and *détournements*, he feels, anticipated the tactics of Narrative design, by a pinball machine. Yet he eschews the aleatoric, infinite open-plan of Constant's 'New Babylon' for play with rule and transgression, and when there is no given architectonic framework, he is happy to adapt and subvert a classical format; indeed, even to use, as in the chaos of Tokyo, a classical form as a subversive exception to that city's 'natural' mode.

An exedra, borrowed from Palladio's Teatro Olimpico, structured Coates' 1978 Millbank Housing project. Here, the fanshape of Siena's great Piazza del Campo models a 'private public realm' in a city without a European tradition of civic space. The Forum is a staging of communications events in a theatre of artificial landscapes, but in a milieu whose terms oscillate like

Hotel Otaru Marittimo

Galla Chair

its curving tectonics: the 'action' is in the auditorium, the 'scenae frons' is an adjacent railway viaduct. Formats are never fixed for Coates, but invite variance and 'difference' (in Derrida's double sense). The exedra was there already in 'ArkAlbion', a 1984 reinvention of a ruined County Hall as a new kind of civic complex of public and private exchange, but Coates lined it with builder's bin-chutes, a symbolic 'order' for a city of endless renewal.

For his Bastille Opera, Coates imagined 'a huge railway shunting yard' for set-wagons. In front of this an enormous wall running from one end of the site to the other. This ties the auditoria to one another and in turn, these to the place. In doing so, it exaggerates the proscenium arch to the scale of a mountain:

> . . . even if it begins as a café and ends as the old viaduct. To the audience the wall plays with emblems of the performance, giant metal Valkyries, old costumes on wires, cascades of musical instruments . . . cloakstores are pulled out of the wall at the start and finish of every performance . . . [4]

THE WALL (relay: *Viaduct*)

A glance at the layouts of even the 'simplest' of Coates' conversions – Caffè Bongo, London shops, the Bohemia jazz club – will show that narrative ideas of intertwining, mutating, and hybriding are fully translated in plans. Yet for Coates, the elevation and section are at least as generative, the more so since in them movements in, through, and across are simultaneously vivid and sensuous. When the city and street are conceived of as continuous interior, then mezzanine, belvedere, and balcony transform their traditional potentials. What ties them together, however, is the line, which may run with the street, or transgress it as viaducts do.

Although narrative design is in the first instance inspired by the graphic life of signs and events, certain forms and types present intrinsic narrative facilities: extensible, flexible arms of airport gates, factory halls and viaduct undercrofts. The wall may be the simplest such facility, offering three parallel conditions in depth – before, athwart, behind – in addition to its dimensions of height and length in which to dispose the triad of place, use and sign, that constitutes the narration of conventional programme. In Tokyo, where elevations work like vertical streets, Coates was invited to design a building that would house a variety of bars and cafés on a narrow site. Such diverse interior uses were likely to come and go whilst the whole building had to last, indeed endure the possibility of earthquakes. If the variety of cafés reflected a global relativism, the perdurance of the structure stood for transcendent time. Coates therefore decided to dramatise this contrast. He placed a giant handwritten billboard on the site, announcing:

> The concept for the building revolves around a wall of monumental proportions – a wall which could have been built by the Romans, a wall of stone and giant arches, a wall which could have encircled cities. But unlike the ruins of Rome, this wall is both ancient and still being built. Sculptures in the form of ancient building cranes suggest that the building is continuing to grow towards the future into the 21st century.

In fact the Wall is threaded with conceits on past, future and change. Two metres thick, it contains lifts and stairs which appear halfway up like a fire escape, accessing floors which cantilever behind it to hold the bars behind a rear wall of frosted glass. It is the front wall, of course, which bears the narrative that mediates street and interior. Rather like the clothes racks at Jigsaw, an iron screen stands proud on the pavement. It could recall a Victorian gasometer frame (it was cast in England) and the antique reference is given another twist by Jessica Thomas' bronze figures swarming up it. Another resemblance is to scaffolding, long an enthusiasm of Coates for intrinsic narrative facility, and as an index of reconstruction. During the 80s, every street in London seemed decorated with the scaffoldings and bin-chutes of refurbishing contractors, busily transforming the innards and uses of buildings which a year or two earlier had been inwardly hijacked and transformed by squatters.

This double kind of unofficial and official mutation had been the theme of the NATO group 'Gamma City' installation at London's AIR Gallery, which they had clad in scaffolding and chutes for its duration.[5] The Tokyo Wall continues this Capriccio on process by casting back as far as the Romans (it was built by Tuscan bricklayers) and forward to its cornice of aircraft undercarriages, recast as if a flying Noah's Ark of the future had landed on the roof and been recycled along with all the previous strata and strada of history.

NOAH'S ARK, Sapporo, (relay: *Strata*)

Boats and planes, rather than motorcars, are Coates' favoured means of motion (though Lambrettas get a look-in). Boats floated into his architecture via the Docklands projects that he ran as tutor of AA Unit 10 in the early 80s, but it was in the 1983 ArkAlbion project that Noah's Flood became an emblem of the renewing wave of narrative architecture, perched atop the Mount Ararat of London's former County Hall. The occurrence of sea fossils on clifftops is a 'natural' narrative in topography (read Adrian Stokes' on limestone in *The Quattrocentro*), but Noah's Ark is surely the 'primitive hut' of narrative architecture. A mountain surmounted by a boat, bearing a house, and filled with global beasties is a veritable *Iconologia* (in Ripa's sense) of Coates' world. The improbable collision of boat and *Berg* is a surreal image, but it figurates the abstract treatment of impacting events that Coates' AA tutor, Bernard Tschumi, deployed in his 'Folies' at La Villette. For Coates, however, the notion of 'event' is anything but abstract, and of all models of narrative co-presence, that of man of beast is most primal. His vision here (and his NATO colleague Mark Prizeman's), is like Rubens' sensuous 'other' of architecture, rife with potential to deconstruct by means of creature *jouissance*. Interestingly, Mark Wigley has to resort to a bio-metaphor in his account of decon-structive design: ' it becomes unclear which came first, the form or the distortion, the host or the parasite. They compose one symbiotic-entity'.[7] The Ark fuses an Etruscan temple with a boat-berg in sprayed concrete around an inner spiral stair. Somewhere in this 'drunken boat' is a sunken tower of Babel – site of broken bonds and sundered tongues: the disseminated raw material of global narrativity, re-fusioned in electronic media.

OTARU HOTEL (relay: *Globality*)
Like Vico, Joyce, and Fischer von Erlach, Coates has been fascinated by modes of recurrence, recycling, and universality realised as linguistic synthesis. A possibility of a fertile microcosm, in which a dream of wholeness might be recovered in cooperative concert enters his journal already in Italy: 'Existential devices – association, occupation – define space or become part of it. This is a painful process. Far too complex for me to define alone.[8] Likewise, the plenitude of the site has recurrently presented itself as a might-be world *in nuce*.

Starting the NATO collaboration, Coates wrote an article on the then-derelict docklands of London's Isle of Dogs, re-visioned by his colleagues as 'Albion', a place of anarchic intervention where 'each building assembles pieces pirated either from a local but deliberately inappropriate source, like a crane or church tower, or from as far away as possible, from the jungle or childhood, or anatomy, or even recent events. But the dereliction was merely a local intensification of potential everywhere:

> Drawn but real: the very self-sufficiency of Albion holds it up as ironic dystopia, yet places it concurrently against the city as given. Even though docklands will turn out to be a dogs' dinner, Albion will be built a little more quietly over a much greater area. Hence it is simultaneously confined and universal, ghetto and globe . . .[9]

Several years later and several thousand miles away, another defunct port provided the site for an allegorical realisation of Coates' microcosm. In a former banking hall, fish shoals and archipelagos sea-change it into a hotel restaurant as

'floating world', havened by guest rooms inspired by ports: Alexandria, Bangkok, Naples. But also many collaborators – if the hotel was an 'encyclopaedia' of sea-cultures, its production was a mix of movie-making and a cast of decorative artists that Von Erlach might have summoned. Narrative design knows no tectonic prejudice; its motifs are prodigal, promiscuous, and inter-subjective; it 'detournes' the decorative through the software of today' the decorative through the software of today's volatile decorum.[10]

TAXIM (relay: *deRELICT*)
A tenet of NATO practice was that Narrative was lived or nothing. Rephrase Wittgenstein: 'Don't ask for the meaning, ask for the *misuse*'. Accordingly, all kinds of transit from ortho to heterodox were catalytic, notably, decay. Ruin and errant reuse were the punk part of NATO. Where Corbusier proposed the pristine *Dom-ino* frame, NATO preferred the skeletal hulk. Taxim began as such a hulk, a derelict Istanbul dyeworks, a concrete frame, a squat. It still exists, a ruin de-relic'd, re-used, but resistant to 'softening'. It is now a 'night-park', that is, a nightclub that recapitulates a garden, indeed doubly, for if a garden is escape to pleasure, still more is night. Many soft devices of seductive narrative are there – catwalk, glass-bead screen, diaphona of gauze and glass, harem ambience of sensuality and Ottoman luxury. Many brash ones, too – the airport disco, airfreight containers as video-bunkers away from the dance, image-projectors and triwonder hoarding. Mutations abound – sofa-mouth-landscape, glass-bead eyes, flux of body language. But across all, the concrete hulk remains as it is – narrative need not flux everything. Sections and plans of Taxim show a frame consuming mobile forms, and organs like the swelling mezzanine devouring the Cartesian skeleton – each thing supplementing, whilst displacing the other. Paradoxically, the orthodox frame here is 'nature' as much as it is 'order', because it remains a ruin, an uncanny negation of disco's urban ecstasy. Narrative is amongst other things, a dialectic of alienation. The whole of Taxim questions the 'whole' of Taxim. An oxymoron: orde/r/uin, it presents an image of a future in ruins and ruins in future. Will ruins exist in future? Or will they have to be manufactured? Not the real thing nor its simulation is what fascinates, but the transit between the two.

LONDON (relays: *Body, Exedra, Viaduct, Strata, Globality, deRELICT, SofTransit*)
Rasmussen's celebration 'London, The Unique City' was flattering but already out of date. Incorrigibly, as resistant to grand ordering as Taxim's frame is to displacement, London has eluded modernism and now looks, in the debacle at Canary Wharf, set to defeat corporate

Never before has there been such active back and forth between individual and organisation, production and consumption. Systems and their signs are our new currency – we're more adept in the virtual space of data

A loss of civic cohesion afflicts all Western cities, from London to Paris, Brussels, to Barcelona: none of these has succeeded in matching its software dimension to the hardware of its physical infrastructure

If physically cities are the sum of their buildings, roads, rooms, tunnels, tracks and towers, more fundamentally they are the societies that live in them, are inspired by them, are taunted and tantalised by them

Distinguish the expressive dimension of architecture with the added-on or in-between. There should be 10% for intermediary architecture. It's time for architecture to be financed separately from buildings

Soft planning – part process-aware urbanism, part architecture, part design, part event devising – will provide the city with overlapping thematic drifts that spur a plethora of complementary variations

monumentalism. Yet it has never lacked vitality in the kind of culture that is uttered, worn, played, or acted. The problem has been to configure this existential environment in a responsive architecture. It may be that beyond the current disillusion, a time is at hand when London's unique mix, neither so formal as Paris nor as prolix as Tokyo, and with a recurrent gift for nurturing diverse surprises, may sponsor its own unique solutions once again. The key is to look at the details on the streets and the whole through the media, and to find the common codes they both articulate.

An early NATO project involved a multicode reading of the Isle of Dogs through its life-patterns and morphology that resembled Roland Barthes' account of reading in *S/Z*.[11] Since 'Gamma City', emphasis has shifted to mutable facilities: Think of an intermediate architecture on that edge between people's lives and the given city, a kind of city furniture poised to refurbish rather than rebuild.[12]

For an ICA exhibition of *Metropolis*, Coates created an eruptive model from junk and multiple metaphor.[13] Called *Eurofields*, it turned derelict railway lands of Kings Cross into a freetrading zone, visioned as 'a blistering electronic countryside'. Ceramic fire components modelled embassies and commodity marts symbolised as 'butter volcanoes', represented in the model by pulsating rubber gearstick casings. 'Interweaving of movements, roads, railways, monuments, overgrown sidings, lines, canals, twisted and grafted with goods and passengers' were depicted in Plasticine, pegboards, radio valves, windscreen wiper motors, and toy trainset, whilst overturned videoscreens announced its programmes in synthesised voices and intermeshed images. The whole model was wrapped around with crash-barriers. Eurofields turned the man-made wilderness of the old railway yards into a landscape just as wild but now doubled with new uses and redoubled as images of exotic terrains – oases, Cappadocian caves, Yemeni towers, cornucopian tents – connoted by puns and spread around the site's Victorian gasometers. Yet Kings Cross was now untypical of London, the last tract of industrial wasteland left in the heart of the metropolis (it may yet remain a waste). It was always clear to Coates that London's renewal had to emerge in sites and situations already protoactive in its daily life. The design task was to early-detect transformative impulses, configure them locally, then relay and propagate at city-scale by an architectural activity that would have more in common with software designing, TV production, and event-staging than traditional planning. As usual, Coates envisaged a double-register to this strategy. On the one hand, there was direct engagement with the new tools:

Customise situations with new means and new technologies, not as futurology but as taking stock. Tape decks, disc-drives, and VTRs have outgrown their status as commodities. They're spare parts of the architecture of our daily lives.

On the other hand, an expanded poetics of image and figuration arose in concert, to relate the human and informatic environments:

Use materials to exploit their differences. Bend them, stretch them, paint them, and erode them, use their contortions to build impulses into dynamic form, we want sensual architecture, which stimulates.[14]

Two journalistic manifestos illustrated this re-imagined city. In *London 2010*, we combined specific sites of metamorphosis – Farringdon, towerblocks, Oxford Street, suburban houses, banks and garages – with a panorama of reclad, rewired, and re-iconologised business buildings. No longer bland utilities, and frankly declaring their artifice as urban theatre-sets (a Brechtian 'alienation effect'), they sprouted polysteeples and holograms to act out a continuous civic masque.[15] *London 2066* for *Vogue*[16] took the relay on to a stage when 'there are no monuments as such, but soft-monuments, parts of the city that work as urban icons, with their activity, process, and light'. By now, Coates' *London Narratised* has become visionary, biochemical, electronic, mythic; the dialectic of enlightenment has come full circle, recycled all alienation into a *Cyclopaedia of imaginative facility, a Codex of renewable resource.*

Through a process of 'ecstacising' shifts and transformations that combines logical steps with intuitive leaps, a new urban landscape evolves from the given condition

Explore the potential of the river as both park and city resource. There will be fountains, sculptures, temples and pavilions. But instead of woods and lawns read water, instead of paths read gangways and jetties

The Ecstacity proto-project focuses on the Strand-Fleet St. axis and its parallel, the Embankment. It exploits the suspended disbelief of the white gallery to host a dreaming of the civic core of London

Here London is not so much a map of boxes as a complex organism of interactive layers and compositions. Many of these include radically disparate parts, they are deliberately hybrid and heterogeneous

Interactive parts form themselves into architectural conditions that test and compliment existing buildings: memories of the old city are brought to life by a cyber architecture that has grown in its cracks and open spaces

Notes

1 N Coates, *Architectural Positions* for *Harvard Review.*

2 B Hatton, *Configuring Mercurius: Code To Capriccio*, in *ArkAlbion And Six Other Projects*, Exhibition Catalogue, Architectural Association, 1984; cf B Hatton, *A Collideoscope, Or Real Allegory*, AA Files No 9, 1985.

3 R Poyner, *Nigel Coates, The City in Motion*, Blueprint Monograph 1989, p 19.

4 *ArkAlbion, op cit.*

5 N Coates, undated message to CIA Tokyo, in Poynor, *op cit.*

6 NATO 3: Apprentices, Architectural Association 1985, cf B Hatton, *Produkti For Metamorpolis*, AA Files 12.

7 M Wigley, *Deconstructivist Architecture*, MOMA, NY, 1988.

8 *Configuring Mercurius, op cit.*

9 N Coates, *Ghetto and Globe*, NATO 1: Albion; AA 1984.

10 See B Hatton, *Arcadia and Epicommedy: The Architectures of John Outram And Nigel Coates*, in *Ottagono* 94, Milan 1989.

11 Configuring *Mercurius, op cit.*

12 N Coates, *Gamma Theses* in NATO 3, AA, London, 1985.

13 *Metropolis* Exhibition catalogue, Institute of Contemporary Arts, London, 1988.

14 *Gamma Theses, op cit*, cf N Coates, *Street Signs* in *Design After Modernism*, ed J Thackara, Thames & Hudson, 1988.

15 The *Observer* Colour Supplement, 31 December 1989.

16 *Vogue*, June 1991.

Jigsaw

*OPPOSITE: Jigsaw, Brompton Rd,
London, 1991
RIGHT: Jigsaw, High St Kensington,
London, 1988*

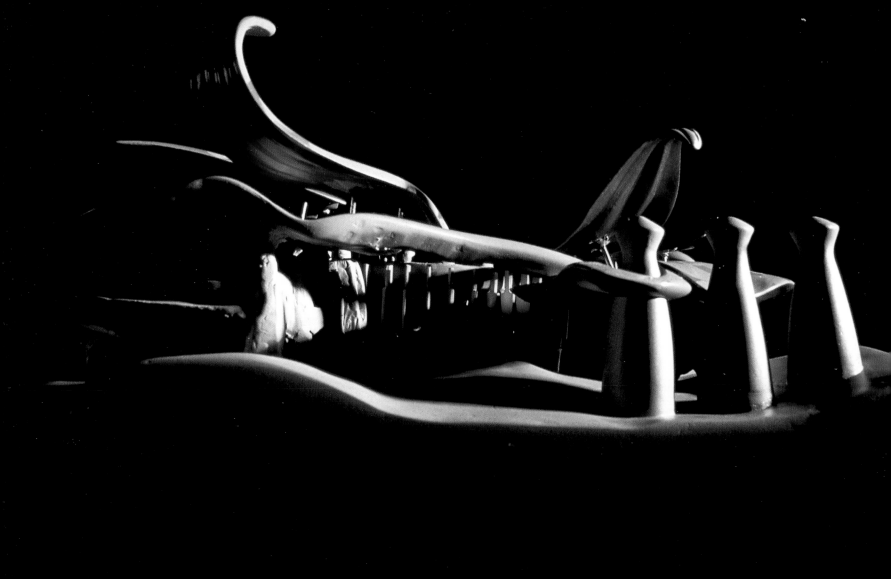
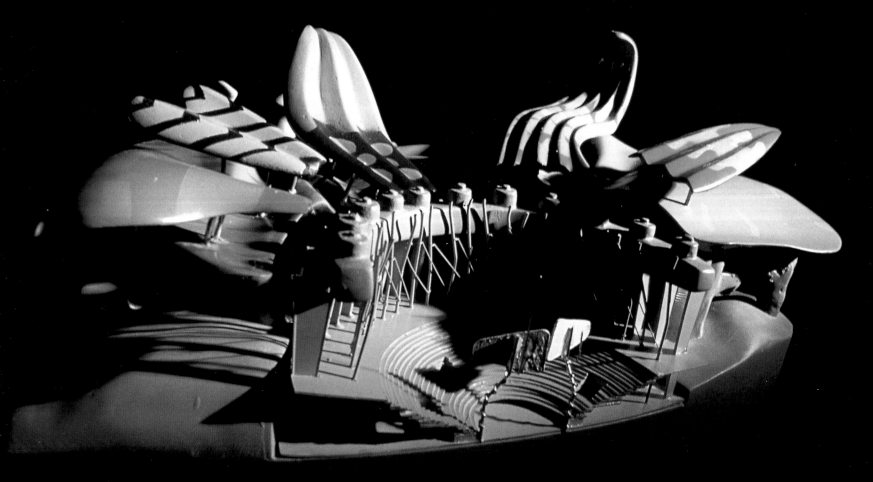

Tokyo Forum

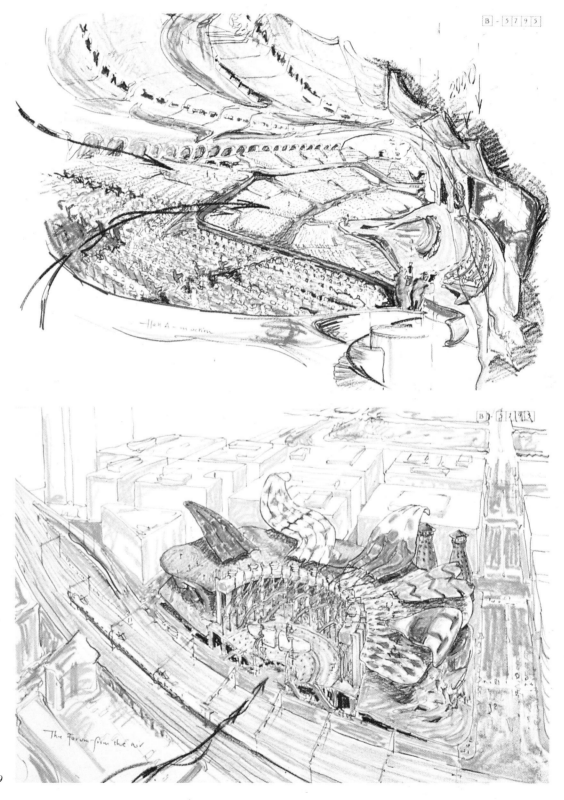

Tokyo Forum Competition entry, 1989

Noah's Ark

E Valentine Hames

E Valentine Hames

E Valentine Hames

Nishi Azabu

Noah's Ark, Sapporo, 1988

Kings Cross

The Wall

The Wall, Tokyo, 1990

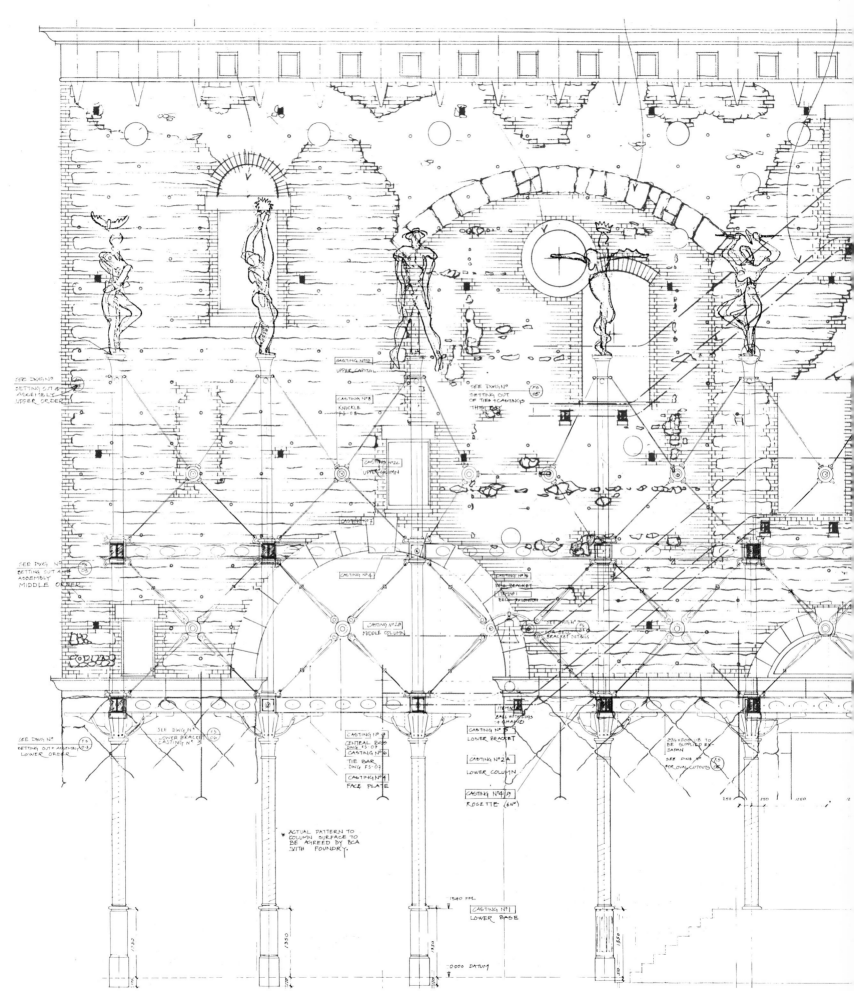

OPPOSITE: Penrose Institute, Tokyo, completion, 1993
ABOVE: The Wall, Tokyo, 1990

Hotel Otaru

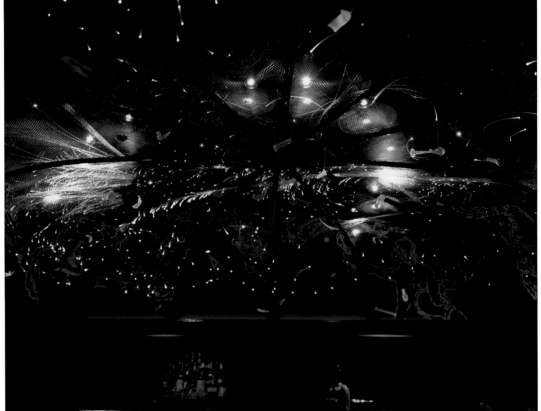

Hotel Otaru Marittimo, Otaru, 1989
ABOVE: 'Engine Room' Discotheque
BELOW: 'Star Bar'

E Valentine Hames

Furniture

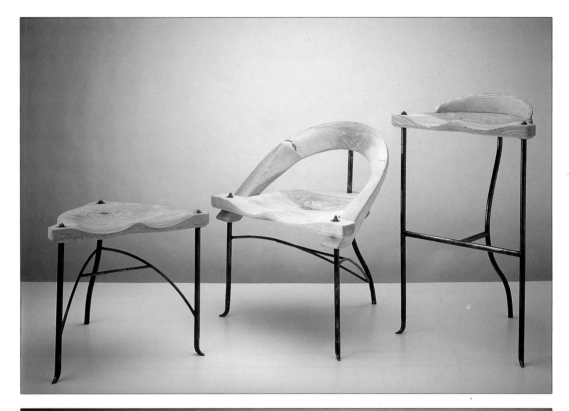

LEFT: Galla armchair, Poltronova Design, 1989
ABOVE: Noah Collection, SCP Ltd, 1988
BELOW: Delfino Wardrobe, Arredaesse, 1991

Poltronova Design, SCP Ltd. Arredaesse and Omniate